T&T CLARK STUDY GUIDES TO THE NEW TESTAMENT

THE LETTERS OF JUDE AND SECOND PETER

Series Editor
Adrian Curtis, University of Manchester, UK

Other titles in the series include:

T&T Clark Study Guides to the Old Testament:

LETTERS OF JUDE AND SECOND PETER

An Introduction and Study Guide
Paranoia and the Slaves of Christ

By
George Aichele

Bloomsbury T&T Clark
An imprint of Bloomsbury Publishing Plc

B L O O M S B U R Y
LONDON · OXFORD · NEW YORK · NEW DELHI · SYDNEY

Bloomsbury T&T Clark

An imprint of Bloomsbury Publishing Plc

Imprint previously known as T&T Clark

50 Bedford Square	1385 Broadway
London	New York
WC1B 3DP	NY 10018
UK	USA

www.bloomsbury.com

BLOOMSBURY, T&T CLARK and the Diana logo are trademarks of Bloomsbury Publishing Plc

First published 2012. This edition published 2017

British Library Cataloguing-in-Publication Data
A catalogue record for this book is available from the British Library.

ISBN: PB: 978-0-5676-7111-0
ePDF: 978-0-5676-7113-4
ePub: 978-0-5676-7112-7

Library of Congress Cataloging-in-Publication Data
A catalog record for this book is available from the Library of Congress.

Series: T&T Clark Study Guides to the New Testament, volume 19

Cover design: clareturner.co.uk

Typeset by Newgen Knowledge Works (P) Ltd., Chennai, India

FOR CONNIE

CONTENTS

ACKNOWLEDGMENT

Unless otherwise noted, the English translation of the Bible cited in this book is the Revised Standard Version (1971). The Greek text of the New Testament is from Nestle and Aland (1979).

Portions of the Preface were first published in my book, *Jesus Framed* (Routledge, 1996), Chapter 5. Portions of Chapter 2 were read to the Reading, Theory, and Bible section of the Society of Biblical Literature at its 2010 Annual Meeting in Atlanta.

I thank Tat-siong Benny Liew for encouraging me to write this volume for the series, and Fred Burnett, Peter Miscall, Raj Nadella, Robert Seesengood, Richard Walsh, and especially Benny Liew, for numerous helpful bibliographic and other suggestions. Any flaws in the book are my own responsibility.

NOTE

A brief Glossary of unavoidable technical terms used in this book may be found following the Preface.

[T]he vision of all this has become to you like the words of a book that is sealed. When men give it to one who can read, saying, 'Read this', he says, 'I cannot, for it is sealed'. And when they give the book to one who cannot read, saying, 'Read this', he says, 'I cannot read' (Isa. 29.11-12).

PREFACE: THE VIEW FROM MARS

> [H]owever discontinuous language itself may be, its structure is so fixed in the experience of each man that he recognizes it as a veritable *nature*: do we not speak of the 'flux of speech'? What is more familiar, more obvious, more natural, than a sentence read? (Barthes 1986: 94, his emphasis).

In a short essay, 'The Advertising Message' (1988), Roland Barthes imagines the case of a Martian – that is, 'someone from another world'. This Martian knows the vocabulary and syntax of 'our language' quite well, but she is 'utterly ignorant' of human culture. Barthes's Martian is 'deaf' to metaphor and other connotations, all the nuances and shades of verbal meaning that are attached to words in the various ways that they are used, through specific cultural codes. Nevertheless, as long as any communication from Earth contains 'here on this first level, a sufficient set of signifiers and this set refers to a body, no less sufficient, of signifieds' (1988: 174), then this Martian will be able to receive 'a perfectly constituted message'.

'Signifier' and 'signified' are technical terms used by scholars such as Barthes. The signifier is the material stuff of a sign, such as a word, and the signified is a thought or concept associated with that sign. (For definitions of all the technical terms used in this book, see the Glossary.) In other words, the Martian is able to understand any sentence in 'our language' only in terms of clear, straightforward connections between the signifying material of its words and some meaning. Consequently, her understanding of this message is hopelessly 'literal', and she is 'stupid' in regard to any other information that might be inferred from the utterance by anybody with a broader experience of the human world – for example, nuances or overtones of words, slang or idiomatic usage, or local or group-related variations of meaning, all the connotations that are for most of us taken as 'obvious'. For Barthes, the Martian's understanding of the message defines the 'analytical character' of the denotation of its words as distinct from their connotations.

'Connotation' and 'denotation' are technical terms for subdivisions of the signified. The denotation is the object or feeling that the sign points to, and the connotation is what the sign implies about whatever it denotes.

Barthes presents more technical and less fanciful discussions of connotation and denotation elsewhere in his writings (for example, 1967a: 89-94). He admits that the concept of pure denotation is 'utopian' (1983: 30), and this would imply that the Martian's naïveté can only be approximated as an extreme, impossible limit. Barthes even speaks of a 'mythology' that associates Mars with impartial judgment: 'Mars [is] merely an imagined Earth, endowed with perfect wings, as in all dreams of idealization' (1979: 28).

In other words, there is a problem with the concept of denotation even in this imaginary form. How could the Martian, or anyone, understand a human language but have no understanding of the culture or history through which that language has been formed? Even though language seems very 'natural' to the adult, fluent user, there is nothing natural about it. No one could learn vocabulary and syntax, whether as an infant or through study of an additional language, unless through that very process she acquired some understanding of the cultural, social, and historical matrix in which that language is inevitably and inextricably embedded. As a result, denotation is inconceivable apart from connotation. Words and sentences cannot clearly denote objects or events without drawing upon fields of 'sense' (another word for connotation) even though sense itself is often fluid, subjective, and even unconscious (see further Deleuze 1990).

In this way Barthes turns the traditional understanding of the denotation-connotation relation on its head. Denotation has usually been regarded as the primary level of linguistic meaning, the bedrock of correspondence to reality on top of which secondary layers of connotation can be built. In this more traditional understanding, denotation provides the 'vehicle' that supports the 'tenor' of any metaphor, the 'primary' or 'literal' meaning (the 'dictionary meaning') to which nuances are often added. Barthes inverts all of this and shows that denotation is instead a degenerate form of connotation, a sort of crippled language. Denotation is 'raw' language, crude and untenable (Barthes 1977: 62-63). Therefore 'denotation is not the truth of discourse: ... [but rather] a particular, specialized substance used by the other [connotative] codes to smooth their articulation' (1974: 128). In the terminology of logic, the extension (denotation) of a word is determined by its intension (connotation), and not vice versa (Copi and Cohen 2005: 105-107). In other words, the 'dictionary meaning' does not define a word, but rather it is defined by how that word is used.

Barthes contrasts the analytical character of denotation to the 'total message' of connotation, which in the case of advertising messages always means only one thing: buy me! Every ad for every product connotes just this one thing. However, Barthes's Martian reader will always be mystified by this element of connotation. For the Martian, the advertising message is simple and innocent, but utterly misleading, for the denotations of advertising messages are always trivial and only their connotations are of any importance. As Barthes says of poetry, which is also usually rich with connotations,

> The Word is no longer guided *in advance* by the general intention of a socialized discourse; the consumer ... receives [the word] as an absolute quantity, accompanied by all its possible associations (1967b: 48, his emphasis).

'The Word' in this quote refers to any bit of language that might have more than one meaning, and not specifically to the Bible. Nevertheless, the connotative mystification that the Martian feels in relation to the advertising message is evident in relation to each of the biblical texts, and especially texts such as the letters of Jude and 2 Peter, each of which is rich in connotation and poor in denotation.

Connotation turns the signified message into a double message which 'disconnects' the denotative meaning and thereby supports an illusion of 'naturalness'. Barthes calls this the 'innocence' of language (1986: 65-66). Nevertheless, even though the specifics of denotation no longer matter in language that is as highly connotative and 'innocent' as the advertising message, they are indispensable. Despite the crippled functioning of denotation without connotation, there can be no connotation at all without denotation. Thus in some respects the traditional understanding of denotation and connotation remains valid. The apparently natural quality of the advertised object arises from the culturally-determined symbol-system that denotation appeals to through the sequence of words, even though this 'naturalness' is itself a product of connotations.

> The excellence of the advertising signifier thus depends on the power ... of *linking* its reader with the greatest quantity of 'world' possible: ... experience of very old images, obscure and profound sensations of the body, poetically named by generations, wisdom of the relations of man and nature, patient accession of humanity to an intelligence of things through the one incontestably human power: language (1988: 177-178, his emphasis).

Barthes concludes that the advertising message, in its use of connotation, serves as the paradigm of *all* narrative. What is true of the advertising message is true of every story, to one degree or another. It is certainly true of the entire contents of the Bible, not only the stories but also the poetry, proverbs, legal codes, and letters such as Jude and 2 Peter. In these biblical texts, the meaning has been delivered from the primary level of denotation but then returns all the more powerfully at a secondary, connotative level. However, the advertising message differs from many biblical texts in at least one important way: most advertisements are explicit about their own double-ness. As Barthes says, 'the second signified (the [advertised] product) is always exposed unprotected by a frank system, i.e., one which reveals its duplicity, for this *obvious* system is not a *simple* system' (Barthes 1988: 178, his emphases). The advertising message says one thing and means another, but it also says, quite 'frankly', that 'this message means something else'. Very few biblical texts are such 'frank systems'.

Only a fool or a child pays serious attention to the advertisement's deno-tations – or a Martian. The Martian of Barthes's essay reads the advertise-ment in absolute isolation from any historical, literary, and cultural tradi-tions to which it has been bound. She is a reader from 'the outside', not unlike those people to whom the gospel of Mark's Jesus addresses the para-bles 'so that they may indeed see but not perceive, and may indeed hear but not understand' (4.12). Like the advertising message, almost none of the language of the Bible can be taken at face value – or rather, if it is read in a strictly and exclusively denotative manner (if that were even possible), the canonical sequence of words, sentences, and books generates a wild multiplicity of inconsistent and contradictory meanings, some of which are outrageous or quite bizarre. This is why the absolutely naive reader of the Bible (like the Martian, a limit case, but also necessarily an outsider) is unable to understand its language.

In contrast, the Christian reader often has no difficulty understanding the Bible's language as rich with theological and narrative significance, just as the consumer in modern Western civilization has no difficulty under-standing advertising messages. Christians are not Martians in relation to the Bible. Some Christians may claim to believe that the Bible is 'literally true', but they do not read it in the Martian way. Corresponding to the cul-tural conventions that lend to the advertising message its quality of natural-ness is an elaborate set of theological conventions that enable the reader of the Bible to encounter its texts as though they were transparent – even perhaps as though the Bible 'speaks for itself'. The Christian reader uncon-sciously reads biblical texts as though they 'naturally' and clearly identify the 'Word of God' and the 'Gospel of Jesus Christ'. This can only happen because connotations are hard at work. The believing reader is aware of many of the text's connotations – she is not one of 'those outside' – but she is often unaware of the connotative duplicity. She knows how she is sup-posed to read the Bible.

It is widely believed by many Christians that only they properly read and understand the scriptures as the single Word of God, which is the one Gospel of Jesus Christ. In other words, true faith is an essential ingredient for correct understanding. Despite this, many non-believing readers of the Bible also encounter its passages as though their meaning is clear, espe-cially those readers who have been sufficiently enculturated with general-ized 'Christian values'. These values continue to play a large role in Europe and the Americas, and thanks to mass media and the global presence of Euro-American culture, they are now readily accessible even to peoples and cultures in a great many other parts of the world. Although these values are increasingly secularized and the Christian element in them has been watered down or is questionable, nevertheless these readers, like their Christian counterparts, all 'know' what the Bible 'says'.

What confuses the Martian and distinguishes every connotation from denotation is ideology. The signified of every connotation, says Barthes, 'is at once general, global and diffuse; it is ... a fragment of ideology' (1967a: 91). 'Ideology' is itself a word that has many connotations, but I understand ideology not as a set of beliefs (as many do) but rather as the way that a person (or group of people) puts her (their) beliefs together, and how that assemblage enables her (them) to live in the world. In relation to religion, ideology often takes the form of theology, both the more explicitly organized concepts of church doctrine but also the sense of self and world implicit in any believer's faith.

Ideologies are generally shared with others, like languages or cultures, and you learn your ideology in the same way that you learn your native language and your 'own' culture. Everyone has an ideology, and it influences everything that you hear, think, and say. Ideology is often largely unconscious, and it is not voluntary. You cannot choose your ideology, and you are always caught up in it. You can change it, but that often involves a difficult and painful process of self-examination. Ideologies arise from the fact that humans are finite, fragile beings, deeply immersed in their worlds, and their knowledge of anything is always partial and limited. There is no escape from ideology, and there is no ideology-free knowledge of anything. Even the ideal of objective scientific or historical knowledge is itself a product of ideology.

As a result of the relation between ideology and connotation, every encounter with a text is driven by ideology. Texts acquire meanings that seem obvious and natural and unquestionable to some people, even though these meanings are not at all obvious to others, thanks to differences of ideology. Despite the claims of many, no text can ever speak for itself. Neither denotations nor connotations are already there in the text, to be dredged out carefully by perceptive or expert readers. Any written text by itself is just ink marks on paper or pixels on a screen, and any spoken text is just vibrations in the air. They are all meaningless until someone reads them, juxtaposing them with other texts and thereby filtering them through an ideology.

It is possible to achieve some degree of critical awareness of your own ideology, and this may happen when you become aware of other ideologies offering other options, other truths than your own. This may also happen when a text resists your attempts to make sense of it, not so much by presenting another ideology but by contesting or disrupting your beliefs, encouraging you to become conscious of them or even to rethink them. At that point you may start to 'read from the outside'. You then become something like Barthes's Martian reader.

The Martian reader knows nothing about the Bible, the Word of God, or the Gospel of Jesus Christ. She does not know who wrote any of its books, or where or when. Many of the biblical texts say nothing about these matters, and even when they do – as both Jude and 2 Peter do – there is reason to doubt their claims. Nor does the Martian know who read the biblical books when they were first written, or who has read them since, or how any of its readers have understood them. If she receives the Bible as a compendium of books, she does not know why these particular books are bound together, or why others have been excluded. Nor does she know why the included books are arranged in two Testaments, or why they are arranged in a particular order in each Testament. The Bible itself never explains any of that.

The Martian reader does not read all these books as conveying the Word of God, much less as all denoting or connoting a single message, such as a sequence of historical events, or the Christian Gospel. Instead (for example), in the four biblical books called 'gospels', which are not the same as the Gospel, the Martian reads four different stories about four different Jesuses (and their followers and enemies), and for her it is not clear what any of these Jesus simulacra might have to do with each other, or with the Jesus Christs who appear in the letters of Jude and 2 Peter, or the one in the letters of Paul (see Aichele 2011). For the Martian, as Barthes said in a passage that I quoted earlier,

> The Word is no longer guided *in advance* by the general intention of a social-ized discourse; the consumer ... receives [the Word] as an absolute quantity, accompanied by all its possible associations (1967b: 48, his emphasis),

and this time let us pretend that 'the Word' refers to the Bible. The Bible, like poetry or advertising, is rich in connotations, which the Martian does not understand.

This is why the Martian's reading is utopian, as Barthes says, but this is also why I admire the Martian and seek to emulate her in my own reading. I do not want to be, nor do I think I can ever be, free of ideology, but I do want to be critically aware of the effects of ideology on my own readings and the readings of others. As a result, my strategy is to read texts such as the letters of Jude and 2 Peter as problems, to treat them not as answers or solutions but as questions or puzzles. I do not think that there a single clear message in the biblical texts to be faithfully, transparently transmitted – but this only means that the text is all the more perplexing, and thus more worthy of study. I invite my readers to read from the outside, stupidly, as I try to do, and not to assume that they already know what the text means, or that someone else does.

GLOSSARY

The following is limited to terms that are used in technical or highly specific ways in this book. See also the 'guide' to vague or potentially confusing phrases in the letters of Jude and 2 Peter that appears in the Appendix at the end of Chapter 1.

Canon: a standard or rule. In relation to texts, a collection that is thought to be complete and exclusive, such as the works of a particular author. Applied to the Bible, it describes the complete collection of essential texts ('scriptures') for Christian reading and worship.

Codes: cultural filters through which the reader understands a text.

Connotation: also known as 'sense' or 'intension'. The wider meaning of a term, often (mistakenly: see the Preface) thought of as a second or indirect layer of meaning that is added on to the layer of denotation, as in a symbol or metaphor.

Denotation: also known as 'reference' or 'extension'. The ability of a term to 'point' directly to an object or idea, often (mistakenly: see the Preface) thought of as the primary level of meaning.

Ideology: the way in which someone's ideas come together in their thoughts and actions to form a more or less coherent whole. A system of beliefs that is shared to some extent with others. Theology is ideology in relation to religion.

Intertextuality: meaningful similarities and tensions between texts, the 'space' of reading in which meaning appears. A form of ideology.

Paranoia: as used by Gilles Deleuze and Félix Guattari, this term refers to a semiotic regime or discursive formation in which there is rigid control over the flow of meaning.

Source text: in translation theory, the text that is to be translated.

Schizophrenia: as used by Gilles Deleuze and Félix Guattari, this term refers to a semiotic regime or discursive formation in which the flows of meaning are uncontrolled.

Signified: the mental or conceptual aspect of a sign. The meaning of the sign, which may be either connotation ('sense') or denotation ('reference').

Signifier: the physical aspect of a sign, such as written marks, sound waves produced by a voice, or pixels on a computer or television screen.

Simulacrum: a concept or virtual object, the reality effect of a text produced by intertextuality.

Target text: in translation theory, the text that results from the act of translation.

1

CRITICAL ISSUES IN JUDE AND 2 PETER, OR WHAT THE MARTIAN MAY NOT KNOW

[T]he valorization of sameness always already presupposes difference as its source (Castelli 1991: 122).

[G]ood and holy men ... also breed on scraps and remain stuck to the fragments which they carry away (Deleuze 1986: 130).

Codes and Canon

The reading of any written text draws upon a variety of culturally-acquired codes or filters, through which the reader sorts the signifiers to decipher the meaning or signified of that text (see Barthes 1974). Most of these are codes of connotation, and therefore the Martian reader who was described in the Preface is largely unaware of them. As human beings, we begin to learn such codes when we learn to understand and speak our 'native' language(s) as infants. At first they are basic codes to decipher verbal signifiers and connect them to signified meanings. Then we learn more codes as we become increasingly immersed in the societies and culture(s) in which we are raised. We learn even more codes as we learn to read – codes required by the technologies of writing – and then still more of them, such as the ones necessary for literary, scientific, or historical understanding, through other processes of formal education.

Because of the need for such codes, no text can speak for or by itself. The meaning of any given text results from the inevitable tensions between that text and other texts which arises in the understanding of the reader. These tensions are sometimes called 'intertextuality', and the range of this intertextuality is always much broader than the explicit citing of one text by another. Because many of these codes reflect the reader's ideology (which is discussed further in the Preface; see also the Glossary), in relation to reading texts, ideology takes the form of intertextuality.

These codes and processes of intertextuality direct the understanding of any written text. In regard to the Bible, the reader often draws upon codes that are grounded in cultural and other forms of knowledge more specific to her experience and understanding of Christianity, and ultimately, through her own private experience with other texts, both biblical and non-biblical. However, the most powerful influence on this reading is usually the intertext that is provided by the Bible itself, as the 'canon of scriptures' (see Aichele 2001). For Christian (and even many non-Christian) readers of the biblical scriptures, probably the most powerful context for understanding any of them, including the letters of 2 Peter or Jude, is provided by the Bible, understood as the single 'Word of God'.

Desire for a Christian canon first appears in the second century CE, when Christians began to make lists of writings that were acceptable for use in worship. Apart from 2 Peter (see 3.15-16) and a few other New Testament texts such as Eph. 2.20, desire for a canon first appears with Marcion, whose own, narrow selection of texts was itself eventually rejected by other Christians, in part because Marcion rejected the Jewish scriptures. Somewhat later in that century, Irenaeus argued in favor of limiting the group of accepted gospels to only Matthew, Mark, Luke, and John, and Origen accepted the letters of Paul, the Revelation, and several other letters (including probably 1 Peter) in addition to the four gospels. The document known as the 'Muratorian Canon', which is regarded by many (but not all) scholars as coming from the second century, provides a more complete list, which includes Jude but not 1 or 2 Peter.

However, it is not until the fourth century, with Eusebius and Athanasius (and perhaps also the Muratorian Canon, if it is dated later), that the entire New Testament as it is now known appears in lists of the accepted canon, and this is when the oldest more or less complete Bible manuscripts also first appear, as far as we know. Even then and for some centuries afterward, the contents of Christian Bibles (and canon lists) vary considerably. In other words, just because there is evidence of desire for a canon, it does not follow that a canon is already in place, or that a uniform Bible is widely used.

Although different Christian groups disagree about the exact extent of the canon, there is a great deal of overlap between the different canon lists. In addition, although the canon was never officially 'closed' by any church, most churches regard it to be effectively closed. In other words, books cannot be either removed from it or added to it, at least not by individual readers. The canonical books are identified as 'scripture' – that is, as more authoritative than other writings. As the list of all those books that Christians are expected to regard as worthy of reading and use in worship, the biblical canon is therefore a very powerful intertextual mechanism. The canon signifies the unity and totality of the Bible, as the 'Word of God'. It holds the Bible together, and apart from it, there is no Bible as such – even if the books are still bound together in one cover – but merely at best a collection of books which may or may not have anything to do with one another.

The biblical canon assembles a list of specific and otherwise disparate books that should be read together, so that they may illuminate and clarify each other as they are read. Because individual written texts cannot speak by themselves, one purpose of the Christian canon is to form a complete set of texts that will in effect 'speak for itself', at least in the hands of faithful readers. The canonical control of meaning does not appear in the individual texts themselves but rather in the ways in which the texts are juxtaposed with one another in the reader's interpretive practice. In this way the canon reveals the Word of God to the believing reader, directing the reader's understanding of the books contained within it.

However, this canonical control mechanism does not always work very well, and as a result, confusion and varying interpretations are always possible, and frequently occur. Additional codes for understanding these texts are provided through the worship, teaching, and other activities of the various Christian churches, and these often include codes that come from long traditions of Christian as well as Jewish reading of the texts. Finally, modern scholarly study of the texts in their historical, literary, and cultural contexts offers even further codes for their understanding.

The ideology embedded in the intertextuality of the biblical canon frequently and heavily influences the reading of its books. That influence is often evident in the ways that readers read the letters of Jude or 2 Peter, and each of those books in turn plays an important role in the ideology associated with the Bible and the theologies derived from the Bible (see Chapter 4). The biblical canon in effect provides a field of 'correct' reading, authorized by Christianity. It is inherently exclusive:

> The texts we call 'the New Testament' are collected under the sign of 'canon', a term oscillating between self-authorization ... and the concomitant de-authorizing of alternative knowledges which are more or less systematically degraded, debased, and eventually all but completely destroyed in the creation of the authoritative text (Castelli 1991: 49).

In other words, the canon is an exercise of Christian authority, and since 'authority' is a matter of great interest in both Jude and 2 Peter, along with the meaning of the 'scriptures', this may have influenced the decision to include each of these letters in the Bible.

Tucked away near the very end of the New Testament, the letters known as 2 Peter and Jude are so small that they are easy to miss altogether if you are flipping quickly through a Bible. Jude is divided into 25 verses and not further divided into chapters. Second Peter is divided into 61 verses, which are further divided into three chapters. These books are often ignored by biblical scholars (Martin Luther called Jude 'a neglected letter', see Martin 1994: 81-82, especially n.24), partly because they provide very little specific information about the communities to whom they each were addressed or about the opponents whom they each attack. However, I suspect that they are also ignored because many biblical scholars are at least a little bit embarrassed by what J.N.D. Kelly calls their 'general mediocrity' and 'denunciatory tone' (1969: 223). For although the language of each letter is striking and colorful, the general tone of both of them is one of deep fear and suspicion, not between Christians and 'the world' (as, for example, in 1 Peter), but within two early Christian communities.

Although both Jude and 2 Peter are now included in the canon of the scriptures, each one apparently had some difficulty getting into the it. Ancient Christian thinkers such as Tertullian, Clement, and Origen, all in the second century, regarded the letter of Jude as acceptable, but the church historian Eusebius, in the fourth century, listed the book as 'disputed'. Jude's problems were apparently mainly tied up with its reliance on the non-canonical book of *1 Enoch*, but also with the question of its authenticity – that is, doubts regarding whether the letter had really been written by the brother of Jesus and James. This question of authenticity will be discussed further below. One of the principal criteria for a text to be considered canonical in the New Testament was its 'apostolicity' – that is, was the book written by one of the known apostles of Jesus, or someone closely associated with an apostle? Later, during the Protestant Reformation, Jude's value (along with the books of Hebrews, James, and Revelation) was again questioned from various points of view by men as different as Erasmus, Luther, and Cardinal Cajetan. Luther even put Jude (as well as Hebrews, James, and Revelation) in an appendix at the end of the Bible. The letter of 2 Peter was not so much disputed as generally ignored in the ancient world, at least by commentators, but Origen had doubts about the letter and Eusebius among others rejected it (Leaney 1967: 100, Kelly 1969: 224). Near the end of the fourth century, the Christian theologian Didymus the Blind described 2 Peter as a forgery and non-canonical.

Authors, Dates, Locations

Throughout this book, I will refer to each of the authors of these letters as 'he', since that is evidently the gender that each of them wants to project. However, when I use the terms 'Jude' or '2 Peter', that will be in reference to the texts of the letters, and not to the persons who wrote them. Each letter begins with a clear statement of its author's name and his claim to authority ('brother of', 'apostle of'). Nevertheless, both the authorship of Jude and that of 2 Peter have been in doubt ever since at least the second century, and they still are.

The letter of Jude's author begins by identifying himself as 'a servant of Jesus Christ and brother of James', and this may not seem like much help, since both 'Jude' (*Ioudas*, Judas or Judah) and 'James' (*Iakōbos*, Jacob) were very common men's name in Jewish families, as was 'Jesus' (*Iēsous*, Yeshua or Joshua). There may well have been many sets of brothers named Judas and Jacob in the first centuries of the Common Era. Luke 6.16 lists 'Judas the son of James' as one of the disciples (see also Acts 1.13), and several other Judases are mentioned in the New Testament, including most famously, Judas Iscariot.

However, there was one very well known Judas–Jacob pairing in the early Christian movement, and that was Jude and James, the brothers of Jesus (Matt. 13.55; Mark 6.3; see also Matt. 27.56; Mark 15.40). The introduction to the non-canonical gospel of Thomas identifies its writer as 'Didymos Judas Thomas', implying perhaps that Judas was the twin brother of Jesus (see Cameron 1982: 23-24). It is widely assumed that the opening of the letter of Jude implies that its author is no less than the brother of the messiah, Jesus, as well as of James. According to the Acts of the Apostles, James was a leader of the early Christian movement in Jerusalem, after the death of Jesus (12.17; 15.13; 21.18), and this understanding is supported also in the letters of Paul (1 Cor. 15.7; Gal. 1.19; 2.9, 12) as well as the gospel of Thomas (12). According to the Jewish historian Josephus, Jesus' brother James was martyred in Jerusalem in the year 62. However, apart from the letter of Jude and a minor tradition about his descendants, Jesus' brother Jude is not alluded to any further (but see 1 Cor. 9.5).

Biblical scholars are divided between those who believe that the brother of Jesus did really write this letter (see Bauckham 1983: 14-16) and who tend to date the letter to the middle of the first century CE (when that brother might still have been alive), and those who are very doubtful or deny outright that the letter was written by the brother of Jesus, and who tend to date the letter considerably later, at the end of the first century or in the second century. The former group of scholars also tend to be conservative Christians who for theological reasons argue that the Bible is reliable and accurate (or even infallible) in what it says, and perhaps because of this, they tend to read these letters in a more positive light. The latter group tend to be more liberal Christians or non-Christians who are not commited to the inerrancy of the biblical texts, and who are also less likely to be charitable in their treatment of this letter.

If the author of Jude is identifying himself to be the brother of James and Jesus, then the opening of the letter immediately raises questions, for the author does not call himself the brother of Jesus, but rather 'a servant [*doulos*, slave] of Jesus Christ' (1.1; see Leaney 1967: 81-82). The author is not being modest here (although the early theologian Clement of Alexandria suggested as much), for he does not hesitate to claim the derived authority of being the brother of James. The New Testament letter of James, which is traditionally attributed to James the brother of Jesus but also widely thought to be pseudonymous, similarly begins with its author claiming to be 'James, a servant of God and of the Lord Jesus Christ', although in James there is no mention of any brothers.

Perhaps to claim the status of brother to the 'Master and Lord', as Jude 4 calls Jesus, would be saying too much. Jude's self-identification may even reflect some notion that Jesus was miraculously conceived, as in the story in Lk. 1.26-38 (see also 3.23), and therefore that neither its author nor his brother James could be Jesus' full brothers. The gospel of Luke does not list the names of Jesus' brothers (see 8.19-20), and the Acts of the Apostles (widely believed to be Luke's sequel) does not identify James as a relative of Jesus.

However, neither the gospel of Matthew, which hints at the virginal conception of Jesus (1.18, 20), nor Mark, which does not, gives any indication of that belief in their lists of Jesus' brothers, both of which include James and Jude. Furthermore, that Jude's author believes in the virginal conception of Jesus seems doubtful for other reasons (see below and Chapter 2). Perhaps Jude and James are just another set of brothers with the same names, in which case the identification may have helped when the letter was first circulated, if the recipients knew them, but it is now of no value or even misleading.

In addition, it is doubtful that the letter was written by Jesus' brother Jude for other reasons. This letter is written in elegant Greek, 'closely woven in artistic shape' (Martin 1994: 67), and therefore suggesting a relatively well-educated author. If Jesus' brothers were the sons of a Galilean carpenter (so Matt. 13.55), they were probably not literate. Although it was not impossible for a Galilean peasant to become a skilled writer of fluent Greek, it is more probable that if a brother of Jesus knew Greek at all, it would be rather limited, ad hoc Greek, since Galileans were sometimes in contact with Greek-speaking people (as in Mark 7.26). Perhaps more decisively, the letter of Jude refers to 'the apostles of our Lord Jesus Christ' (v. 17) not as the friends or associates of his own brothers but as though they are other people, perhaps in the past (Kelly 1969: 281; see also 354), and both Jude and 2 Peter seem to reflect a time period in which Christian doctrine has become relatively settled – it has become 'the faith which was once for all delivered to the saints' (Jude 3) – even though the particular doctrine(s) in question may not always be clear to the reader. This would suggest a date in the second century, when Jesus' brothers would very likely be dead.

In addition, Jude shows little or no evident interest in an impending destruction of the world, a theme that often appears (although in various ways) in the earliest Christian writings, and if 'the last time' in Jude 18 suggests a time when the imminent return of Christ was no longer expected (see Kelly 1969: 282-83), then it also implies a writing date at or after the end of the first century. Finally, a relatively late date is also suggested by the absence from either Jude or 2 Peter of any hint of tension between Jews and gentiles in relation to the Christian movement, which plays a large role in Paul's writings and is at least a factor in each of the gospels. There is no evidence to support any specific location for the writing of the letter of Jude, although speculation tends to favor a more or less 'Jewish Christian' community or communities in Syria or Palestine (but see Kelly 1969: 292-93).

Almost the entire letter of Jude appears in 2 Peter, mostly in that letter's second chapter. In his commentary on Jude and the epistles of Peter, A.R.C. Leaney nicely summarizes the options for a historical relationship between Jude and 2 Peter. As Leaney notes, if a common source (analogous to the alleged Q material 'behind' the gospels of Matthew and Luke) were supposed for the similar material in the two letters, 'we should find it nearly identical with Jude' (1967: 77). Similarly, Kelly claims that 'There is indeed hardly anything in Jude which does not reappear in some form in 2 Peter, so that the supposed common source must have been to all intents and purposes identical with it' (1969: 226).

Therefore it is highly probable that one of the letters copied the other, and 'if 2 Peter was the first to be written, Jude must have extracted the middle and taken this as his basis' (Leaney 1967: 77). In that case, why some material had been extracted and other material discarded would then have to be explained. However, this extraction option is 'less likely than that 2 Peter expanded Jude by the addition of further material' – which is the simpler hypothesis to explain – and Leaney then proceeds to demonstrate why this is so with detailed examples from the two letters (1967: 78-80; see also Kelly 1969: 330). In other words, you can suppose that Jude was derived from 2 Peter if you want, or even that they were written independently, but it will be far more cumbersome to do so. In addition, Jude does not specifically mention Peter as an apostle, and this counts against any idea that Jude was a rewriting of 2 Peter. That 2 Peter rewrote Jude will be explored in considerable detail in Chapter 3.

There is less debate among scholars about the pseudonymity or authenticity of the letter of 2 Peter than there is about Jude, probably because 2 Peter's evident dependence on Jude would by itself raise serious doubts about its authenticity, apart from the evidence that suggests a relatively late date of writing. In any case, 2 Peter begins by identifying its author as 'Simeon Peter, a servant [*doulos*] and apostle of Jesus Christ' (1.1), and the author later claims to have been an eyewitness to some event involving Christ that may have been the transfiguration, or possibly the resurrection (1.16-18). There is none of the ambiguity of Jude's self-identification, although 'Simeon' (rather than 'Simon') is rather odd in a Hellenistic context (Kelly 1969: 296). If James was indeed the successor to Peter as the leader of the Jerusalem Christians, then 2 Peter's claim may even be an attempt to 'trump' Jude's apostolic insinuations.

Terrance Callan notes several shifts in verb tense between the two letters, from aorist in Jude to future in 2 Peter, and he attributes these to 'the fiction that the author is Peter, writing in the past' (2004: 44). The author of 2 Peter claims to be nearing his death, 'as our Lord Jesus Christ showed me' (1.14), and this may have added to the weight of his words. He also claims to have written an earlier letter (3.1), but whether this is the biblical text known as 1 Peter is very doubtful, and this too has been doubted at least since Origen. Although the letter's author may know the letter of 1 Peter, it is unlikely that he wrote it, as there are significant stylistic discrepancies between them (Ehrman 1997: 394; Kelly 1969: 235-36), as well as major differences of focus and emphasis.

Modern Christian readers are sometimes bothered by allegations of pseudonymity or pseudepigraphy in relation to biblical writings, perhaps because the implication of human deception is considered to undermine the divine authority and reliability often ascribed to the Bible. However, it is well know that pseudonymity and pseudepigraphy were common phenomena in the ancient world (see Leaney 1967: 111; Ehrman 1997: 320-23), as was plagiarism (such as 2 Peter's apparent appropriations of Jude), and these activities were not at that time considered morally inappropriate in themselves. This does not contradict what I said above about the problems that Jude and 2 Peter had with getting into the Christian canon. The fact that a text is pseudonymous does not make it any less worthy to read. However, canonical status was determined in part by a text's claim to an apostolic pedigree, and pseudonymous apostolicity would not be enough (see Kelly 1969: 224).

Nevertheless, if both Jude and 2 Peter are pseudonymous texts, as seems highly likely, then that might imply that their authors were unknown to the first readers of those letters. Pseudonymity has little authoritative value if 'everyone knows' who really wrote the text. 'Read this letter as though it were written by the brother (or the disciple) of Jesus, and pay no attention to your own knowledge that it really wasn't' sounds rather like the 'doublethink' made famous in George Orwell's novel, *Nineteen Eighty-Four* (2003). If the authors of Jude or 2 Peter were indeed known to the addressees, as many scholars seem to think, then what would be the point of the pseudonyms?

A poem attributed to 'Shakespeare' may retain its aesthetic value after it has been conclusively proven that William Shakespeare could not have written it, but only as long as the author remains unknown, or is identified as another well-known poet, such as Christopher Marlowe. If instead it is discovered that the poem was written (perhaps as a prank, or for fraudulent purposes) by one who wrote only imitations or forgeries, then it may quickly lose its interest. In the case of Jude and 2 Peter, the fact that we don't know who wrote them does not necessarily detract from their respective theological values. Given the evidence that suggests that the brother of James and Jesus did not write the letter of Jude, then it seems probable either that its first recipients did not know the author, or else that he is indeed someone named Jude with a brother named James whom they did know, but not the famous brothers of Jesus. In the case of 2 Peter, however, there are fewer options.

The very likely dependence of 2 Peter on Jude implies a date for the writing of that letter even later than that of the letter of Jude, probably well into the second century, and thus probably long after the death of the disciple Peter. Since 2 Peter's author evidently regards at least some of the letters of Paul as 'scriptures' (3.15-16), this coheres well with the idea that the letter was written in the second century, when Paul's letters were becoming widely known. Second Peter also conjoins 'the holy prophets' and 'your apostles' (3.2) in a phrase that hints at something like the Old and New Testaments (see Chapter 3). As I noted above, it was during the second century that desire for a Christian canon first becomes evident. To this evidence should be added 2 Peter's struggle against 'false teachers' (2.1) over doctrinal purity and that letter's attempts to develop arguments justifying the non-occurrence of the *parousia* (3.3-15, see Chapter 3).

Once again there is no reason to assign one location for the writing of 2 Peter rather than another. Kelly favors a gentile Christian community in either Egypt or Asia Minor, but he notes a wide range of other options (1969: 237; see also Callan 2001a: 257). Ralph P. Martin argues more narrowly for a 'member of the Petrine school', probably in Rome (1994: 139; see also 145-46, apparently following Bauckham 1983: 327-30). The addressed community is somewhat familiar with the Jewish scriptures, but the influence of Hellenistic thought on 2 Peter's language is also strong. The Greek of 2 Peter's text is fluent, although somewhat pompous and awkward; Callan describes it as in the 'grand Asian style', which he compares to the baroque (2003: 223; see also Martin 1994: 135). However, as Kelly says, '"Peter" for all his pretentious flights is a conspicuously careless stylist' (1969: 360), and this is perhaps most evident when 2 Peter is compared to Jude.

Terminology Matters

In both Jude and 2 Peter, the name 'Jesus' has become inseparable from the title 'Christ' (*christos*: messiah, anointed one). The name is never simply 'Jesus', except for 2 Pet. 1.2, and even there it is 'Jesus our Lord'. Otherwise,

'Jesus' never appears apart from 'Christ', and vice versa: they have become a single name, 'Jesus Christ'. This combined name is quite common in the New Testament epistles and the book of Acts (230 times, although sometimes it is 'Christ Jesus', as in the letters of Paul), but it is rare in the gospels (5 times) and in Revelation (3 times).

In addition, in both Jude and 2 Peter 'Jesus Christ' is quite often further modified by the addition of the title 'Lord' (*kurios*). Jude consistently uses the larger phrase 'Lord Jesus Christ' (or variants such as 'Jesus Christ our Lord'), and 'Jesus Christ' apart from 'Lord' only appears twice, both times in verse 1. The same is true for 2 Peter, with 1.1 being the only exception. Second Peter also frequently calls Jesus 'Savior' (1.1, 11; 2.20; 3.2, 18; see also 3.15), but this term is reserved in Jude for God (v. 25). Although the gospels of Luke and John do identify each of their Jesus simulacra as 'Lord' or 'Christ' on various occasions, the combination of 'Jesus' with both 'Christ' and 'Lord' never appears in the biblical gospels or Revelation. Furthermore, although 'Lord Jesus Christ' or its variants appears often in the New Testament letters and Acts, of the 72 total instances, 10 of them are in the letters of Jude or 2 Peter, a rather high percentage for these two tiny texts.

This highly consistent identification of Jesus Christ as Lord may suggest that each of the Jesus Christ simulacra of these letters is characterized as God, since 'Lord' is often used as a euphemism for God in the Jewish scriptures, and the phrase 'only Master' (Jude 4, compare 'only God' in v. 25) often connotes monotheism in Jewish or Christian texts (Kelly 1969: 252). A few ancient manuscripts of Jude even make this identification of Jesus with God explicit. However, neither Jude nor 2 Peter ever clearly identifies Jesus as a divine being, and 'Lord' can also be used as a term of respect and deference for human beings (for example, Mark 7.28).

Furthermore, in Jude 1, 4, 21, and 25, God and Jesus Christ are both mentioned, but in ways that clearly distinguish them. It is not clear whether God or Christ is the one who acts to save and judge in Jude 5-9, but the distinction between God and Jesus and the word's usage elsewhere in Jude suggests that the 'Lord' who is mentioned without further designation in verses 5 (saving the people out of Egypt in the Greek text, but rendered 'he' in the RSV, see Kelly 1969: 255), 9 (rebuking the devil), and 14 (coming with holy myriads to execute judgment, in the quote from *1 Enoch*) is Jesus Christ, and not God. In other words, 'Lord' is only used in the letter of Jude to refer to Christ. To be sure, if Jesus Christ 'saved a people out of the land of Egypt', then he is not a normal human being, or else 'Egypt' should be read symbolically. A binitarian or even trinitarian understanding of a relation between God and Christ is not excluded by the text of Jude (see Kelly 1969: 243, 285, and Boyarin 2001), but it is not strongly supported by it either. That the words 'Jesus', 'Christ', and 'God' all appear instead of 'the Lord' in these passages in ancient manuscript variants indicate that early scribes were trying to make sense of (and disagreeing about) Jude's language.

In 2 Peter, the relation between God and Jesus Christ that is suggested in 1.1 is unclear, although Callan argues that this verse identifies Jesus as God (2001a: 253; see also 255-56). However, it is also possible to read 2 Pet. 1.1 as referring to two distinct beings (see Kelly 1969: 297-98). Several early manuscripts of 2 Peter even have 'our Lord and Savior' instead of 'our God and Savior' at 1.1, which supports this distinction and reduces the potential for confusion (see Ehrman 1993: 266-67). In addition, Bart Ehrman notes a single, very early manuscript (Papyrus 72, from the third century) that 'corrects' both 2 Pet. 1.2 and Jude 5 to the effect that each of these verses explicitly identifies Christ as God (1993: 85-86). Again, these considerable manuscript divergences suggest that early readers were disagreeing strongly about these matters.

In any case, it does not follow from the fact that both Christ and God are called 'Lord' in 2 Peter that Christ is understood to be God, unless there is only one being who can indisputably be called Lord. (Otherwise, this would commit the well-known logical fallacy of the undistributed middle term. For example, I may call my employer, a stranger on the bus, and a policeman 'Sir', but that does not mean that they are the same person.) This is not clearly the case in 2 Peter, in contrast to Jude, which calls Jesus Christ 'our *only* Master and Lord' (v. 4, emphasis added). Callan argues that 2 Peter distinguishes between Jesus as the son of God and God proper, and he says that this involves 'the influence of Greek thought on Jewish monotheism' (2001a: 261; see also 255, 258). In 2 Pet. 1.17, 'Lord Jesus Christ' receives 'honor and glory' from 'God the Father', which strongly implies a distinction. Elsewhere in that letter, God and Jesus are discussed separately, and 'Lord' may sometimes connote either one, as Callan also notes.

In addition, both Jude and 2 Peter describe Jesus Christ as 'Master' (*despotēs*: slave-owner). Only these two letters in the entire New Testament use this word in reference to Jesus Christ, 'the Master who bought them' (2 Pet. 2.1; see also Jude 4). In Lk. 2.29, Acts 4.24, and Rev. 6.10, *despotēs* connotes God. In 1 Tim. 6.1 and 2, 2 Tim. 2.21, Tit. 2.9, and 1 Pet. 2.18, this word connotes human slave-owners. Thus 'Master' can also be used either in reference to God or in reference to human beings, not unlike 'Lord'. (See further Chapters 2 and 3.)

Satan, or the devil, is never mentioned in either letter, except in passing in Jude 9 (contrast 1 Pet. 5.8). Angels are mentioned in both letters, but again in passing (but see Jude 10 and 2 Pet. 2.10). While both letters are very much concerned with falseness, corruption, and ungodliness, the source of this evil is consistently located in faithless human beings and worldly passions. In addition, although 'Jesus Christ' is very much at the center of each letter, what qualifies Christ to be the Lord and Master is never stated. No mention is made of the death or resurrection of Jesus (contrast 1 Pet. 1.3; 2.24; 4.1), or of his life and teachings, except for 2 Peter's apparent allusions to Jn 21.18-19 in 1.14 and to something like a transfiguration story in 1.16-17.

Numerous other figures of speech or intertextual allusions pepper these two letters. Some readers may find them to be vague or confusing, and they are frequently drawn upon in interpretations of the texts and analyses of either the addressed community of Jude or 2 Peter or its opponents. I present a guide to the more significant instances of this language in the Appendix to this Chapter.

The Good Guys

The letters of Jude and 2 Peter are among those New Testament writings traditionally classified as 'Catholic' or 'General Epistles' (which also include the three letters of John, the letter of James, and 1 Peter). Although 2 and 3 John do seem to have specific addressees, in the other catholic epistles, as in Jude and 2 Peter, there is no specifically identified recipient. This contrasts sharply to the letters of Paul, which are addressed to 'the churches of Galatia' or 'the church of God which is at Corinth' and so forth. It is widely supposed that the catholic letters were intended to be circulated widely from church to church throughout the ancient world, and thus in effect they were addressed to all Christians. However, neither 1 John nor James looks very much like an actual ancient letter, and apart from their openings and closings, whether Jude and 2 Peter were actual letters is also doubtful. While Paul's letters discuss specific issues or incidents in various Christian communities or involving specific individuals (Philemon and Onesimus), the threat posed by the opponents in either Jude or 2 Peter remains vague, despite the abundance of vivid metaphors and scriptural allusions.

Michel Desjardins rightly resists the tendency among scholars to regard the addressed communities as more or less orthodox Christians, claiming that there is not enough evidence in either letter to support such assumptions:

> The common procedure among scholars is first to take a sympathetic or believer's stance to the letters [of Jude and 2 Peter] – that is, to make the authors' concerns and points of view their own, to treat them as 'orthodox', and to continue to place the critical eye on the 'dissident' position. There is also a second stage to virtually every analysis of the dissidents. This is the attempt to find a suitable first- or second-century group with which to identify these 'ungodly' members (1987: 92).

Callan's analysis of the christology of 2 Peter, noted above, serves as an example of this tendency, as it strives mightily to rescue 2 Peter's letter for Christian orthodoxy and even suggests that the letter takes an initial step on the way to trinitarian thought (see also Kelly 1969: 304). The efforts of Kelly among others to distinguish between 2 Peter's use of the word 'knowledge [*gnōsis*]' and that of the gnostic heretics (1969: 298-99) is another example.

Since most of the scholars who discuss these letters are themselves more or less mainstream Christians – that is, they read the Bible 'from the inside', they are definitely not Martians! – they tend to assume that the addressed communities must be those whose beliefs (and scriptures) eventually developed into the variety of early Christianity that became the dominant one when the church in Rome received imperial recognition in the fourth century – that is, what Ehrman calls proto-orthodox Christianity (see further 1997: 6-7, 162-69, 393-96; this is sometimes called 'early Catholicism'). After all, whether Jude or 2 Peter were actually circulated as letters or not may be unclear, but these letters did eventually somehow become widely enough known and accepted to be admitted into the canon of the New Testament. In other words, they were regarded by at least some early Christians as orthodox.

However, it does not follow from their eventual canonical status that the writers and first readers of these letters were themselves proto-orthodox. Indeed, the letters of Jude and 2 Peter say remarkably little about the lives or beliefs of their first readers or intended recipients, and the little evidence that they offer, if they are read independently of the canon ('from the outside'), does not strongly support the view that these recipients were proto-orthodox. In addition, there is no reason to assume that a single community, or two closely related communities, are addressed by Jude and 2 Peter. Instead, the letters provide fairly good reasons to think that these communities are significantly different from one another. That there are important distinctions to be made between these communities appears when one looks closely at 2 Peter's 'rewriting' of Jude, which I will do in Chapter 3.

Anyone who has ever been involved in any sort of political action or organization knows that it is true that 'politics makes strange bedfellows'. It is often overlooked but no less true that religious movements also make strange bedfellows, and that is perhaps especially true for Christian groups in the early centuries of the Common Era. It is now widely accepted that there was no single, united, homogeneous early Christian movement, and thus we also should not assume that any single Christian group was united on matters of faith or morality. Indeed, the letters of the New Testament offer ample evidence that they were not. As a new religion promising salvation for anyone, Christianity attracted a wide variety of people, including Jews as well as pagan 'god-fearers' (Ehrman 1997: 258) and adherents of various Hellenistic mystery religions or philosophical schools, and there is good reason to think that some early Christian groups had a diverse membership.

Despite this, insofar as these communities are described at all in the letters, they display important similarities. Frequent references to 'Jesus Christ' and 'God the Father' indicate that the communities are Christian in some way. Both of these communities apparently regard themselves as slaves of the 'Master', who is Jesus Christ (Jude 4; 2 Pet. 2.1), and in 2 Peter this concept is strongly connected to an apocalyptic understanding of salvation. The concept of Christ as slave-owner sets both of these groups apart from other early Christian communities, at least insofar as the New Testament texts depict them. However, there is a difference between the two letters in their respective appropriations of this concept, and this difference is crucial to other differences between them. I will explore that difference further in the next two chapters.

In addition, both Jude and 2 Peter acknowledge the power of the Holy Spirit, and although at the time of their writing they cannot yet be called 'trinitarian', it is easy to see how they could eventually be drawn upon to support trinitarian thought. Furthermore, both of the addressed communities believe in prophecy and angels. They are apparently familiar with the Jewish scriptures, especially the Torah and at least some of the prophetic books. Although no canon of the scriptures, Jewish or Christian, existed at the time that these letters were written, Jude's community is also aware of texts that were eventually regarded as extra-canonical by both Jews and Christians, *1 Enoch* and the Assumption of Moses, and they may even regard these texts as scripture. Martin suggests that Jude cites *1 Enoch* because it is the scripture of the opponents and in order to use it against them (1994: 84). Such an argument would nicely excuse Jude from violating canonical boundaries, but it would also then require that we distinguish carefully between Jude's message and that of *1 Enoch*. The community to which 2 Peter is addressed may not know these non-canonical texts, but they do regard the letters of Paul and perhaps other Christian texts as scripture, a sort of proto-New Testament. In addition, they are familiar with pagan Hellenistic concepts such as Tartaros.

Finally, both Jude and 2 Peter speak of struggles within the addressed communities between faithful followers of the 'Lord Jesus Christ' and others 'who long ago were designated for ... condemnation' (Jude 4) because they 'exploit you with false words' (2 Pet. 2.3). Desjardins claims that these communities are reluctant to get involved in the larger world or to have any dealings with outsiders (1987: 98), perhaps because they regard that world as a place of immorality, corruption, and error. He also argues that the addressed communities value sexual continence (1987: 97-98), but differing views are argued by Leaney (1967: 122) and Countryman (2006: 749-52). Neither Jude nor 2 Peter suggests any of the trappings of incipient church organization that appear in some other New Testament epistles (such as 1 Tim. 3.2, 5.17, or Tit. 1.7), but both communities apparently practice baptism, for rejection of a second repentance is implied in both letters, and they share in 'love feasts', although these feasts may be another point of difference between the two letters (see Chapter 3).

Desjardins claims that the language of the letters that describes the opponents really tells the reader more about the addressed communities (1987: 96). These communities are very likely autocratic and place a high value on the authority of apostolic founders such as Jude (or his brothers) and Peter: 'The members of these communities ... probably were expected to follow the teachings of their leaders as they would Jesus himself' (1987: 97). Elizabeth Castelli makes a similar point about Paul's letters:

> The discourse of the privileged speaker (Paul, for example) creates the contours of the social experience of early Christian communities. This is often worked out in struggle, as the ferocity of Paul's rhetoric at certain points makes clear. ... The diffusion and specificity of the social groups that called themselves Christians are replaced by a singularity of purpose and a universalism, both of which undercut and indict particularity and difference (1991: 56).

Castelli's discussion of Paul's exercise of 'pastoral power' (1991: 122-24), using a concept derived from the philosopher Michel Foucault, generally applies quite well to the rhetoric of control in both Jude and 2 Peter. She notes that 'In New Testament writings, this form of pastoral power appears again and again' (1991: 47). According to Castelli, Foucault understands pastoral power to consist of four factors:

1. It aims 'to assure ultimate salvation in the next world'.
2. It both commands the community but is also willing to sacrifice itself for the community's salvation.
3. It oversees not only the community as a whole but each of its members.
4. It is concerned not merely with the choices that people make but with how they think and feel (why they make those choices) (1991: 47).

The system of domination in pastoral power, as analyzed by Foucault, refines what Friedrich Nietzsche called 'slave morality' or 'bad conscience' (see 1967: 36-43, 84-85, 167). It is a major factor in Paul's letters, as Castelli shows, and crucial to his relations to the recipients of those letters. However, although neither Jude nor 2 Peter displays the theological sophistication of Paul's letters, pastoral power is perhaps even more prominent (or at least more heavy-handed) in what Martin calls the 'pastoral theology' of Jude, and it is strongly evident again in 2 Peter. Martin summarizes this theology under three points: (1) adherence to apostolic teaching, (2) Jesus as judge, and (3) faithfulness/obedience to God (1994: 75-80, in reference to Jude).

Pastoral power is not simply a matter of some leader having his way, but of the entire community acceding to and participating in some larger interest or purpose, a regime of truth that unites them. For this way of thinking, the community is analogous to a herd (or 'flock') with a 'shepherd' who protects and guides it, and both shepherd and flock are subject to its imperatives. Pastoral power is most explicitly reflected in Jude's phrases, 'our common salvation' and 'the faith which was once for all delivered to the saints' (v. 3), but it also appears in 2 Peter's charge to his addressees to 'confirm your call and election' (1.10) and his claim to have 'aroused your sincere mind by way of reminder' (3.1).

Pastoral power calls for rigorous, continual self-examination to ensure that one is 'doing the right thing', as presented in and by the model (the shepherd). The letters' authors urge the addressees to remain, like each of them, faithful to God ('who is able to keep you from falling', Jude 24; see 2 Pet. 1.10) and steadfast in their slavery to the Lord Jesus Christ. However, Castelli's comment about the letters of Paul applies equally well to both Jude and 2 Peter:

> Just as many technologies of power are constructed to create such self-surveillance, so imprecise exhortations to imitate a model have the dual effect of reinscribing the model's authority while placing the imitator in the position of perpetual unease as to whether she is acting in the proper mimetic fashion (1991: 110).

The vague exhortations that appear just prior to the final blessing in Jude ('build yourselves up ... pray ... keep yourselves', etc., vv. 20-23) and in 2 Peter ('what sort of persons ought you to be', 'be zealous', 'beware', etc., 3:11, 14, 17) offer good examples of this exercise of power by placing readers in positions of 'perpetual unease'. As Ruth Anne Reese argues, by the end of the letter of Jude the reader no longer knows whether she is one of the beloved community, or an ungodly one (2000: 63, 106). Something similar happens in 2 Peter.

The imitation involved in pastoral power invites comparison to the 'mimicry' that has been widely observed in imperial/colonial contexts (see Bhabha 1994; Moore 2000). This mimicry imitates the ways of the foreign colonizer but also transforms those ways in the terms of the colonized people, and the result is 'hybridity'. As Christian communities somewhere in the Roman Empire in the second or possibly first century CE, each of the communities addressed in the letters of Jude and 2 Peter is a 'sub-altern' (non-dominant, and at least somewhat marginal) group. These communities are seeking to maintain their identities in a world composed of many such groups, including probably the nameless opponents and perhaps even each other.

The imperial power, Rome, is never mentioned in either letter, even indirectly (for example, as 'Babylon'), although some Christians may already by the time of 2 Peter associate Rome with the name 'Peter'. However, the threat of destruction from within has apparently been imported from the outside world ('admission has been secretly gained', Jude 4; 'false teachers ... will secretly bring in', 2 Pet. 2.1). In Betsy Bauman-Martin's postcolonial reading of Jude, she notes the mimicry that characterizes that letter's master-slave language and maintains the dominant imperial discourse, but unfortunately she does not pursue the matter (2008: 73-74). Robert Paul Seesengood explores in more depth the language of 2 Peter in relation to a 'fragmented identity, a community unable to agree on what it means to be "Messianic" or "Jewish"' (2007: 38). Seesengood compares this fragmentation to that within the Jewish community as described in Acts 6, which is analyzed in turn by Daniel Boyarin:

> hybridized identities ... need distinction and division. These inner divisions become doctrinal. Some were created by social pressures, some by real physical threat (Seesengood 2007: 39, citing Boyarin 1999).

Seesengood insightfully notes that the Christian orthodoxy that eventually emerges from these power struggles is itself a hybrid system (2007: 42). In other words, orthodoxy (and with it the biblical canon itself) is a 'political' compromise between various divergent beliefs and practices, including those of the authors of and communities addressed by Jude and 2 Peter, and perhaps also their opponents.

The Bad Guys

Pastoral power stands always in reciprocal relation to its own resistance or refusal. In other words, it cannot exist apart from the issues that it addresses: or in theological terms, orthodoxy cannot exist until it defines itself by contrast to heresy. The letters of Jude and 2 Peter imply numerous instances of such resistance, and the relation between these instances and the pastoral power in those communities will be explored further in Chapters 2 and 4.

Although the importance of rhetoric in the language of the letters of Jude and 2 Peter is widely acknowledged (for example, Charles 2008, Joubert 1990, Webb and Watson 2010), only Desjardins has suggested that the descriptions of the opponents in either letter may be exaggerated (1987: 96-97; but see also Callan 2004: 47 n. 14). As Desjardins also notes, correlated with the wide-spread scholarly assumption that the addressees of these letters are proto-orthodox Christians is another assumption: namely, that the opponents must be heretic Christians, and most likely gnostics (1987: 92-93; see also Neyrey 1980: 419). Nevertheless, just as there is no reason to assume that the respective addressed communities are homogeneous, so there is no reason to assume that the opponents described in Jude have the same beliefs and practices as those described in 2 Peter, or even that the ungodly ones described in either letter belong to a single, more or less homogeneous group.

Crucial to the scholarly argument that the opponents are gnostics is the claim in each letter that the opponents are 'licentious' (*aselgeia*, Jude 4, 2 Pet. 2.2, 18). From this it is inferred that these people are 'antinomians' (that is, they recognize and obey no moral law or rule) and therefore gnostics. This licentiousness is an index of the refusal of pastoral power. Desjardins argues forcefully that the blanket identification of gnostics as antinomians is ungrounded. Furthermore, not all antinomians are by definition gnostics. In any case, 'licentious' or 'antinomian' is more the sort of word that would be used to disparage someone of whose behavior you disapprove, such as (to use modern examples) homosexuals, hippies, liberals, or 'savages' – or rather (if you prefer) Republicans, bankers and insurance executives, or lawyers.

A second basis for the scholarly claim that the opponents are gnostics is 2 Peter's reference to 'cleverly devised myths' (1.16), which seems to imply that the opponents are 'following' stories of which the author does not approve – that is, heretical ('other') stories (see Desjardins 1987: 94). Some of the gnostic Christians were known for their elaborate stories (or myths) of numerous heavens and demigods, but like 'licentious', 'myth' is more often a word to be hurled at those who are different or with whom you disagree than it is a word used simply to describe a type of story. Again, much like Paul's rejection of those who preach 'a different gospel' or 'another Jesus' than the ones that he preaches (2 Cor. 11.4), this language tells the reader very little about the beliefs or the stories of the opponents.

Finally, the claim in Jude 19 that the ungodly ones 'set up divisions' is often regarded as a mocking reference to distinctions apparently made by some gnostics between themselves as 'spiritual people' and other Christians as 'worldly people'. Nevertheless, mockery or not, it is the letter of Jude, not the opponents, that makes this claim and sets up these divisions (see Webb 1996: 150-51). Does it then follow that *Jude* is gnostic? In any case, the reader has no way to determine whether Jude's complaint is fair (see Desjardins 1987: 95).

The charge of the opponents' 'licentiousness' in Jude 4 and 2 Pet. 2.2 and 18 suggests that the difference between the believers and the infiltrators is primarily a matter of morality, but the claim that the opponents lack understanding and teach falsely in Jude 10 and 2 Pet. 2.1 and 3 suggests that matters of doctrine may be the main point of contention. Second Peter expresses this latter claim more forcefully than Jude does, with its distinction between 'prophecy of scripture' which can only come from the Spirit of God and is never a matter of 'one's own interpretation' (1.20-21), as opposed to 'cleverly devised myths' (1.16).

However, although this distinction between doctrine and morality is useful for critical analysis, it is also somewhat artificial, for as Kelly observes, in each letter the opponents' 'shameful practices are based ... on a principle' (1969: 230). The fact that the letters state these principles in at best vague or ambiguous language makes them no less important. Indeed, the differing principles adopted by the communities and by their opponents may well be matters of less-than-fully conscious ideology. Although mention of 'the faith which was once for all delivered to the saints' (Jude 3, compare 2 Pet. 1.12) suggests something like a system of doctrine or morality, there is little indication of what it is (see further Chapter 4).

Considered apart from their canonical location and Christian tradition, the letters of Jude and 2 Peter tell the reader very little about the communities to which they are addressed, and they also tell the reader very little about the ungodly others who must be rejected. As Kelly says, 'the heretics are drawn in silhouette, with the content of their teaching only obscurely hinted at' (1969: 226). By omitting this information, each letter opens ways for generalized readings by any group of Christians against any others. It is almost as though these two texts were blank 'form letters', to be filled in with opponents and situations as desired, giving a rather different meaning to the phrase, 'catholic epistle'.

For each of these letters, the two groups within the community may not always be distinguishable, and similarly, it may not always be clear to which group any given individual belongs. Nevertheless, in each case, although the line between the 'good guys' and the 'bad guys' may be faded and hard to trace at points, it is always there, never in doubt, up to the very end. A clear distinction is made between those who believe in the right things and live their lives accordingly, and those who may pretend to do likewise but nevertheless undermine or contaminate the others, and a strong opposition is posited between them, which is the opposition between the norm and the deviant – that is, between those of 'right belief' (ortho-doxy) and the 'others' (heretics). The ungodly ones will always be doomed to the nether darkness, as they always have been, while the righteous ones who have remained faithful will stand before 'the presence of his glory with rejoicing' (Jude 24, compare 2 Pet. 3.14). There is no deconstructive aporia in either letter, and the opposition is maintained. This contributes to the strongly paranoid tendencies in both Jude and 2 Peter (see further Chapters 2 and 3).

Appendix: Some Obscure Language

The comments below should be taken to indicate possible uses of the words or references of the phrases and not as precise or comprehensive definitions or interpretations. Readers wishing more detailed discussion should see a commentary on the letters, such as the concise and reader-friendly one by Leaney (1967) or the more challenging but also much more comprehensive one by Kelly (1969). Readers who know Greek may wish to consult a lexicon, such as those of Walter Bauer (1957) or even better, H.G. Liddell and Robert Scott (1996).

In Jude, but Not 2 Peter

v. 4: 'long ago … designated'. This may refer to (unknown) scriptures, or perhaps to a heavenly book in which God records his judgments of individuals, which is alluded to in the Jewish scriptures (for example, Ps. 69.28; Isa. 34.16). Compare *1 En.* 48.10.

v. 4: 'this condemnation'. This may refer to the letter of Jude itself.

v. 9: 'archangel Michael, contending with the devil'. This may refer to a lost portion of the non-canonical book, *Assumption of Moses*. A similar, but less specific, passage appears in 2 Pet. 2.11.

v. 11: Cain. See Gen. 4.1-15, and compare 1 Jn 3.12.

v. 11: Korah. See Numbers 16.1-35.

v. 12: 'twice dead'. This phrase may reflect early Christian rejection of a second repentance – that is, the belief that baptism is an unrepeatable symbolic death and rebirth from sin and any sin committed after you have been baptized cannot be forgiven. See also 2 Pet. 1.4, 9, and 2.20-22, and compare Heb. 6.4-8.

v. 13: 'wandering stars'. The planets, which are not 'fixed' in the heavens like the other stars, and therefore can be dangerously misleading to night-time navigators. This may also hint at the disobedient angels of Jude 6 (see Kelly 1969: 274). Contrast 2 Pet. 1.19, 'morning star' (see below). A letter attributed to Clement of Alexandria describing the 'secret gospel of Mark' identifies the Carpocratians (early Christian heretics) as 'wandering stars' (see Cameron 1982: 69).

v. 14: 'Enoch … prophesied'. Jude is the only New Testament book to explicitly refer to the non-canonical book of *1 Enoch* (the quote is from 1.9). The passage suggests that Jude and its addressees regard *1 Enoch* as scripture.

v. 17: 'predictions of the apostles'. This may imply that Jude reflects some notion of Christian scriptures in addition to the Jewish ones (Leaney 1967: 129-131). See below on 2 Pet. 3.2.

v. 23: 'the garment spotted by the flesh'. There may be an echo in this Greek phrase (*tēs sarkos espilōmenon*) of the 'blemishes' of Jude 12 and 24, words which also appear in 2 Peter (see below). Martin suggests that this may also connote 'the clothing of the itinerant charismatic prophet ... [or] philosopher' (1994: 75). *Sarks* is a common and often quite significant word in the New Testament, and especially in the letters of Paul.

In 2 Peter, but Not Jude

1.1: 'apostle of Jesus Christ'. The claim to be one of the founding figures of the Christian movement is a very strong claim to authority in the Christian community. This claim is underlined in 1.3-4.

1.6: 'self-control' (twice). See also references to stability in 3.16, 17. This is an important theme in 2 Peter, in strong contrast to Jude, where it is the ungodly ones who 'look after themselves' (v. 12).

1.11: 'kingdom of our Lord and Savior Jesus Christ'. The idea of a kingdom of Christ is unusual in the Bible; elsewhere the phrase 'kingdom of *God*' appears frequently. Whether Christ is equivalent to God in these letters is doubtful.

1.14: 'the putting off of my body will be soon, as our Lord Jesus Christ showed me'. The author's impending death; compare Jn 21.18-19.

1.16: 'cleverly devised myths'. This reference to myths is often cited in arguments that the opponents are gnostic Christians (heretics), but these words may simply mock the opponents' different beliefs (myths as forms of ideology). The Greek word *muthos* can mean 'story', and 2 Peter may be trying to stifle the opponents' stories. See also 2.1, 3.

1.16: 'power and coming of our Lord'. This may refer to the second coming of Christ, but it is closely aligned here and in 1.17-18 with the transfiguration or perhaps with the resurrection (Kelly 1969: 320). See the next entry.

1.16-18: This passage probably alludes to the transfiguration of Jesus. Stories in Matt. 17.1-8, Mark 9.2-8, and Lk. 9.28-36 describe the disciple Peter (along with James and John) as an eyewitness to the transfiguration. However, the mountain is not described as 'holy' in those stories, and 2 Peter does not mention a cloud, or any alteration of Jesus' appearance, unless it is implied by 'majesty' (compare Lk. 9.43). Matthew 17.5 comes closest to reporting the words of the voice as 2 Peter does, and only Matt. 17.6 indicates that anyone heard the voice. Matthew 28.16-20 also describes a meeting of the resurrected Jesus with the disciples on a mountain.

1.19: 'the prophetic word'. The reference is unknown and may just be a general claim that the Jewish scriptures foretell the coming of the son of God, as in 1.17, or more specifically but metaphorically, the rising of the 'morning star' (usually the planet Venus) as the second coming of Christ at the end of the world – that is, the first sign of the anticipated 'day of the Lord' (3.10, 12; compare Rev. 22.16 and see further Callan 2006: 145-148).

2.1: 'false prophets ... teachers'. A widespread concept in the Jewish scriptures: a false claim to the authority of a prophet of God.

2.1: 'heresies' = *hairesis* (choice). While this word often has strong negative connotations, it simply denotes a way of thought or action. Any such objectionable difference is a heresy. See re 'myth' (1.16).

2.4: 'hell' = *tartaroō* (keep in Tartaros). In Greek mythology, Hades is the god whose realm is where all the souls of the dead go, and Tartaros is a pit beneath that realm reserved for those who deserve punishment (see Seesengood 2007: 13-16, Kelly 1969: 258, 331). This Hellenistic reference contrasts with the concept of Sheol in the Jewish scriptures.

2.5: Noah and the flood. See Genesis 6-9. The 'seven others' are presumably Noah's family. Compare 1 Pet. 3.20.

2.7: Lot. See Genesis 19 (and 'Sodom and Gomorrah', discussed below).

2.19: 'slaves of corruption'. Compare 2.12, and 'the secret gospel of Mark': 'boasting that they are free, they have become slaves of servile desires' (Cameron 1982: 69).

2.22: 'the true proverb'. See Prov. 26.11, *Story of Ahikar* 8.18, and compare Matt. 7.6.

3.1: 'the second letter'. Probably an allusion to 1 Peter, which also claims to be written by 'Peter, an apostle of Jesus Christ'.

3.2: 'predictions of the holy prophets and the commandment of the Lord and Savior through your apostles'. This conjunction of the apostles of early Christianity and the prophets of the Jewish scriptures echoes Eph. 2.20 and, even more than Jude, anticipates the two Testaments of the Christian Bible. See above on Jude 17.

3.5: 'an earth formed out of water'. See Gen. 1.1-10, but this was a widespread idea in ancient mythology.

3.8: 'one day is as a thousand years'. See Ps. 90.4.

3.10: 'the day of the Lord'. This theme is found often in the Jewish prophetic writings and suggests a time of judgment and justice. See also 3.12. These verses strongly suggest a cosmic cataclysm and the end of the world.

3.10, 3.12: 'elements'. Stars, planets, anything in the sky between 'the heavens' and 'the earth', sometimes thought to be living, supernatural beings. Alternately, the basic components of the physical universe.

3.13: 'new heavens and a new earth'. This apocalyptic theme is perhaps most fully developed in the Bible in Revelation 21; but see also Isaiah 65–66.

In Both Letters

Jude 4, 2 Pet. 1.3, and numerous other instances: 'ungodly/godly' = *asebēs, eusebēs*. According to Liddell and Scott (1996), *sebēma* is 'act of worship' and *sebomai* is to 'feel awe or fear before God' (see also Bauer 1957, '*sebō*', and Kelly 1969: 302-303). As the prefixes (*a* = 'not', *eu* = 'good') indicate, the ungodly ones lack this quality, and the godly ones have it right. More general terms might be irreverence/reverence, especially toward God. Sometimes 'unrighteous/righteous' (= *adikos, dikaios*) are used to similar effect.

Jude 5, 2 Pet. 1.12: 'remind you'. Apparently the addressees already know all that they need to know. This may also imply that one or both authors are familiar with the addressed communities.

Jude 6, 2 Pet. 2.4: 'the angels'. Probably a reference to the 'sons of God' in Gen. 6.1-4 and the expansion of that story in the non-canonical book of *1 Enoch* (see above re Jude 14).

Jude 6, 2 Pet. 2.4: 'nether gloom'. Another likely reference to *1 Enoch* and its story of the punishment of the 'sons of God' from Genesis 6. This phrase also appears in Clement's 'secret gospel of Mark' letter (Cameron 1982: 69). See also Jude 13; 2 Pet. 2.17.

Jude 7, 2 Pet. 2.6: Sodom and Gomorrah. See Gen. 18.16–19.29.

Jude 11, 2 Pet. 2.15-16: Balaam. See Num. 22–24, 31, and compare Rev. 2.14. On 'Balaam's error', see further Leaney 1967: 92, 123-24 and Kelly 1969: 267-68.

Jude 12, 2 Pet. 2.13: 'blemishes' = *spilas, spilos*. See the various entries for these words in Liddell and Scott 1996 and Bauer 1957, as well as the discussion in Reese 2000: 112-14. See also Jude 24 (in some manuscript variants) and 2 Pet. 3.14 ('without blemish', *aspilous, aspiloi*), and Chapter 3.

Jude 12, 2 Pet. 2.13: 'feasts, carousing' = *suneuōcheomai* ('feast with'). The Greek word appears in both of these texts, but it is translated in very different ways. See Kelly 1969: 269-70, and Chapter 3.

Jude 18, 2 Pet. 3.3: 'scoffers' = *empaiktēs*. The scoffers appear within the quoted prediction in Jude (see above re v. 17) but in the main text of 2 Peter. The quote in Jude 18 is otherwise unknown, as is the one in 2 Pet. 3.4, although the latter is reminiscent of the concern addressed by Paul in 1 Thess. 4.13-5.3.

A Paranoid Gospel: Jude and the Abolition of Difference

There's something happening here
What it is ain't exactly clear ...
Paranoia strikes deep
Into your life it will creep
It starts when you're always afraid
You step out of line, the man come and take you away (Stills 1966).

Wandering stars, for whom it is reserved
The blackness of darkness forever (Barrow, Gibbons, and Utley 1994).

You're Next

At the beginning of the classic science fiction/horror film, *Invasion of the Body Snatchers* (Siegel 1984), a man runs out into a busy California highway, desperately trying to stop the cars while screaming that aliens have invaded his home town of Santa Mira and that 'you're next' (all quotes from the movie are from the videotape, Siegel 1984). He is stopped by the police and taken to see a psychiatrist in an emergency room. It turns out that he is the Santa Mira doctor, Miles Bennell, and most of the movie consists of a single large flashback through which Miles tells his story.

This story begins a few days earlier, when Dr Bennell notices what the local psychiatrist calls an outbreak of 'mass hysteria'. A growing number of the citizens in his cozy rural town have become convinced that their loved ones have been replaced by 'impostors'. Although they look, talk, remember things, and act just the same as they always have, these people just aren't 'themselves'. Later in the film, this mysterious difference is given more detail: these people neither love nor fear, indeed they feel no emotion, and they do not appreciate beauty. Then a friend of Bennell's discovers a strange inert body in his home. The body looks human, but its facial or other characteristics have not yet fully formed: 'it is like a first impression, no features, no details'. The body even has no fingerprints. Soon thereafter, the body begins to wake up, and they see that it has developed a cut on its hand that matches exactly a recent cut on the hand of Bennell's friend.

At this point Miles becomes scared and rushes to the house of his girlfriend, Becky Driscoll, where he discovers bizarre, giant seed pods in her basement and has difficulty waking her from sleep. It is later revealed that the pods grow from seeds that have drifted to Earth from outer space, and they are able to replicate any living organism 'atom for atom and cell for cell'. The replication occurs painlessly while the original person sleeps, and the resulting pod-person lives 'a better way of life, evolved beyond human emotions like hate and love', according to the Internet Movie Database plot synopsis (2010). 'There is nothing to be afraid of', the pod-people eventually tell Bennell. 'We're not going to hurt you'. Now truly alarmed, Bennell tries to contact the police, only to discover that they too have become 'different'. Attempts to make telephone calls to the FBI or state authorities repeatedly fail, apparently because the long-distance phone operators (who were still necessary when this movie was made in 1956) are not cooperating.

By the next morning, it appears that every one of the town's residents has been possessed by the strange pods, except for Miles and Becky, who have forced themselves to remain awake all night. They witness farm trucks filled with the pods arriving at the town square, where the pods are taken by pod-people to place in other locations. 'People have allowed their human-ity to drain away', Miles tells Becky. 'Only when we have to fight to stay human do we realize how precious it is'. After several close encounters with pod-people, Miles and Becky flee the town and hide in an abandoned mine shaft. However, Becky finally cannot keep from falling asleep, and although Miles wakes her after only a few seconds of sleep, it is too late: she too has become a pod-person. She starts screaming to summon the others, and Miles flees alone to warn humanity, returning the viewer to the opening scene and bringing his lengthy flashback to a close.

After hearing Miles's story, the emergency room psychiatrist initially believes that he is crazy, but at the last moment, an injured truck driver is brought in to the same hospital. His truck has been involved in a crash on its way into the city, and it was filled with strange large pods from Santa Mira. The emergency room psychiatrist and the police who brought Miles in are instantly convinced that Miles's story is true, and they rush to send out the alarm. The movie ends, and the day appears to be saved.

The emergency room scenes at the beginning and end of the movie were added to Don Siegel's original cut at the insistence of the film studio. Otherwise the main story would not have been a flashback, and the movie would have ended with Miles standing in the highway, staring straight into the camera, and screaming, 'You're next!' (LaValley 1989: 125). In other words, the finale would have been much darker and less certain. The emer-gency room scenes were removed again when the film was re-released in

1979, shortly after a totally new version of *Invasion of the Body Snatchers*, with an even darker ending, was released (Kaufman 1978).

Siegel's 1956 film is based on the novel, *The Body Snatchers*, by Jack Finney (1998), which was itself originally serialized in *Collier's* magazine in 1954. This film is the first and probably most famous of four movies that have been based on Finney's novel, and it is regularly listed among the greatest movies ever made. Siegel's movie is often regarded as an allegory of the anti-Communist hysteria that was sweeping the United States during the Cold War 'McCarthy' years after World War II and the Korean war. However, despite references to the FBI as the ones who could stop the invasion, both the movie's writer and its director claimed that they intended no allegorical meaning.

Be that as it may, the hysteria allegory cuts both ways: not only are the insidious alien invaders really taking over the town, but the emotional reactions of Dr Bennell and Ms Driscoll seem disproportionate to the transformations of the people, which do not result in obviously horrid or evil monsters but instead explicitly promise a new world of peace and harmony – a world which might, however, amount to something like the classless society. The movie's pod-people are peaceful and apparently wish to do no harm. As one of them explains, the seeds are the 'solution' to people's everyday 'problems'. They only pursue Miles and Becky because they perceive them as a threat to their own species-survival. It would not be terribly hard to read this movie 'against the grain' as 'pro-pod', or at the very least, anti-witch-hunt, even though the entire story is told from Miles's hostile point of view.

Whether the 'body snatching' involves the death of the person involved may be a matter of definition and not of any physical change. In both the 1956 and the 1978 films, the transformation occurs while the original person sleeps. How is this any different than ordinary sleep? None of us wakes up as exactly the same person that she was the previous night, but to say that therefore she died while she slept would be rather odd – indeed, quite paranoid. The 1978 movie develops and clarifies this matter in horrifying detail, in a scene where a seed-pod replaces an original human body after vegetable-like 'intercourse' with it. However, the 1956 movie never explains how the pod-people replace the original people, and the audience of that film simply sees pods bursting open and disgorging nearly-formed inert human bodies, not unlike the body that Miles's friend finds, and similar to unripened vegetables. When Becky 'alters', she simply goes to sleep for a few seconds and wakes up transformed. Nothing visible happens to her body. Whether she or any pod-person could be said to have 'died' is not clear, but she is evidently not some sort of revenant, like a zombie or vampire.

Certainly the terminology of 'body snatching' emphasizes that the process is not voluntary, but then not much about life is voluntary, and to be 'reborn' into a world free of troubles or strife, yet where you can still retain your memories, thoughts, and even your body, does not seem too far from how many people would describe the afterlife. Given the use in the New Testament of words for sleeping and waking (for example, Matt. 27.52, Jn 11.11, and 1 Cor. 15.18-20) as metaphors for death and resurrection (but not always: see Mark 5.39), perhaps an allegorizing of this movie as Christian theology would also be fitting. The story would then depict a sort of rapture – also not a voluntary process – but in this case one that would be entirely this-worldly, and the pod-people would be those who have been saved. However, I am not going to read the movie in that way.

They're Gonna Get You

This intertextual juxtaposition of the movie with the New Testament is not entirely frivolous. Something like the paranoia that permeates *Invasion of the Body Snatchers* appears in the New Testament letter of Jude, and again in 2 Peter, which bears remarkable similarities to Jude and may even be in some ways 'synoptic' with it, much as the gospels of Matthew, Mark, and Luke are said to be synoptic. Indeed, it would be tempting to think of the letter of 2 Peter as a later 'remake' of Jude, analogous to the 1978 remake of the 1956 *Body Snatchers* movie, or Matthew's rewriting of Mark, but I will also not pursue that thought – at least, not much (see Chapter 3).

Jude's brief but richly stylized text is deeply troubled throughout by the possibility of difference among 'those who are called, beloved in God the Father and kept for Jesus Christ' (v. 1). There is some disturbance in the community of the saved (v. 3) which threatens its well-being. In this regard, Jude is anticipated by other New Testament texts, such as Paul's letter to the Galatians ('if we, or an angel from heaven, should preach to you a gospel contrary to that which we preached to you, let him be accursed', 1.8). Apparently subversive agents have infiltrated the Christian fellowship, like the body-snatching seed pods, and they must be stopped. Jude calls upon the beloved community to 'contend for the faith which was once for all delivered to the saints' against others who have 'secretly gained admission, ... ungodly persons who pervert the grace of our God into licentiousness and deny our only Master and Lord, Jesus Christ' (vv. 3-4). Ralph P. Martin argues that the situation described in the early Jewish Christian text, *Didache* (also known as *The Teaching of the Twelve Apostles*) comes closest to describing the infiltrators that Jude attacks. According to Martin, 'itinerant and ecstatic prophets and missionaries are ... making claims for extended hospitality and seeking financial gains, and exerting their influence, especially at the agape meal table' (1994: 83, referring to chaps. 11–13 of *Didache*).

However, despite its vivid language the letter of Jude tells its reader remarkably little about these infiltrators. They are 'worldly people, devoid of the Spirit' who follow 'their own ungodly passions' and thereby cause divisions in the community (vv. 18-19). However, many different 'passions' might divide a community. Unless the reader knows something about the addressed community, these words may merely say that the author doesn't like the way that the others do things. What part of 'our only Master and Lord, Jesus Christ' do these ungodly persons deny? What sort of 'licentious' behavior results when they 'pervert the grace of our God' (v. 4)? This latter is often read as an indication that they are antinomian gnostic heretics, but as I indicated in Chapter 1, that reads a great deal into the text.

In order to understand Jude's objection to the infiltrators, the reader needs to understand the infiltrated, the addressees of the letter. Michel Desjardins argues that Jude says more about this group than about the ungodly ones (1987: 96-98), just as the movie tells the viewer more about the people of Santa Mira (and thereby also ourselves) than it does about the body snatchers. However, the reader is still stymied, for as I noted in Chapter 1, the letter says very little about the 'beloved' community. Jude cites 'the apostles' (v. 17), but no apostles' names are mentioned, which seems rather strange if the author is indeed the brother of James and Jesus. Also referenced are texts from the Jewish scriptures. In addition, an apocryphal book, *1 Enoch*, is drawn upon extensively and specifically quoted (Jude 14-15; see also v. 6 and perhaps v. 4), as well as what appears to be a lost variant from the apocryphal *Assumption of Moses* (Jude 9; see Leaney 1967: 90). However, in contrast to 2 Peter (1.19; 3.4-13), there is no explicit mention of the second coming of Christ or the catastrophic end of the world, even though the addressees of Jude do apparently believe that they are living 'in the last time' (v. 18).

As I also noted in Chapter 1, Jude consistently uses the phrase 'Lord Jesus Christ' (or variants such as 'Jesus Christ our Lord'), never just 'Jesus'. Even the shorter phrase, 'Jesus Christ' (without 'Lord'), appears only twice, both times in verse 1. In addition, the very first time that the phrase 'Lord Jesus Christ' is used in Jude, Jesus Christ is described as 'Master and Lord' (*despotēn kai kurion*, v. 4). Although the Greek word *despotēs*, like the Greek word *kurios*, may be used of either human or supernatural masters, in the New Testament this relatively rare word – *despotēs* appears only ten times, and never elsewhere in combination with *kurios* – is used most often to describe human slave-owners in relation to slaves.

Furthermore, in a passage which may be closely related to Jude 4, 2 Pet. 2.1 also uses *despotēs* to connote Jesus Christ as a human slave-owner, where the word is clearly part of a metaphor for redemption: 'the Master who bought [*agorasantas*] them' (see further Chapters 3 and 4). Since 2 Pet. 2.1 serves as a transition into that letter's second chapter, which as many scholars have noted seems to be a rewriting and elaboration, or as I suggested above, part of a 'remake' of nearly the entirety of Jude's text, this suggests that 2 Pet. 2.1 and Jude 4 may both use *despotēs* in similar ways (see Kelly 1969: 252). These two occurrences are the only times in the entire New Testament that *despotēs* is used to refer to Jesus, and in each case, he is depicted as a slave-owner, and the faithful are his slaves.

In further support of this thought, the letter's author introduces himself as 'servant [*doulos*] of Jesus Christ' in Jude 1, the only place in the entire letter where 'Jesus Christ' appears apart from 'Lord' and the only place in the entire letter where the Greek word *doulos* (servant or slave) appears. This suggests that identifying oneself as Christ's slave is equivalent in Jude to identifying Jesus Christ as 'our only Master and Lord'.

However, the Revised Standard Version translates Jude 1 in a way that seems to weaken this connection. It translates *doulos* as 'servant' and not 'slave', even though merely three verses later Jesus Christ is explicitly identified as 'Master'. In each of the other two New Testament passages where *despotēs* connotes human slave-owners and *doulos* also appears (1 Tim. 6.1, Tit. 2.9), the RSV translates *doulos* as 'slave'. The New Revised Standard Version also makes this distinction, as does the Jerusalem Bible. In contrast, the King James Version translates *doulos* as 'servant' in all of these passages. This sort of differential (and perhaps theologically biased) translation of *doulos* appears blatantly in the RSV of 2 Peter, where the word *doulos* is translated as 'servant' in relation to 'Peter', the purported author (1.1), but as 'slave' in relation to the opponents (2.19). This practice is also adopted in the NRSV, the Jerusalem Bible, and the New English Bible. In contrast, the KJV again translates *doulos* more consistently in both 2 Pet. 1.1 and 2.19 as 'servant', as it does in Jude 1, 1 Tim. 6.1, and Tit. 2.9.

By way of contrast to the master–slave language of Jude and 2 Peter, in Mark 10.44-45, Jesus says to the disciples, 'whoever would be first among you must be slave [*doulos*] of all. For the Son of man also came not to be served but to serve [*diakonēsai*], and to give his life as a ransom [*lutron*] for many'. Similar language also appears in Matt. 20.27-28 and Lk. 22.26-27. In these sayings, anyone who would be first must be slave of all, not just of one master. In addition, in contrast to 2 Peter's 'Master', the son of man does not buy people like merchandise in a (slave) market, as 2 Peter's verb *agorazō* suggests, but instead she ransoms many by giving her life (*psuchē*, 'self') for them (see Aichele 2006: 203-21). She is not the one to be served, but instead she is one who serves.

Although both the concept of 'purchase' and the concept of 'ransom' might fall under the larger theological heading of 'redemption', the ideology (or theology) involved in the sayings in the gospels entails a significantly different understanding of human beings and of salvation than does that of either Jude or 2 Peter. It may not be mere coincidence that the phrase 'son of man' does not appear in either of those letters.

A different contrast, less striking but perhaps more telling, appears between Jude and the letters of Paul. Like Jude, although not as consistently, Paul frequently uses the phrase 'Lord Jesus Christ' (or variants). However, Jude's language of Christ-slavery stands in some tension with the language of Paul's undisputed letters. To be sure, Paul does say that 'he who was free when called [in the Lord] is a slave of Christ' (1 Cor. 7.22; see also 6.20, 7.23), and he speaks of himself as a slave of Christ in Rom. 1.1 and Phil. 1.1. In Eph. 6.6, the author (who calls himself 'Paul', 1.1) also calls on that church to 'be servants [*douloi*] of Christ' (see also Colossians 4.12). However, Paul also says, 'what we preach is not ourselves, but ... ourselves as your servants [*doulous*] for Jesus' sake' (2 Cor. 4.5), as well as (perhaps most deconstructively) 'there is neither slave nor free, ... for you are all one in Christ Jesus' and 'through love be servants [*douleuete*] of one another' (Gal. 3.28, 5.13). In the kenosis hymn of Philippians, Paul even claims that Jesus Christ took the form of a slave (*doulou*, 2.7).

Furthermore, *despotēs* never appears in the undisputed letters of Paul, and this suggests that Paul's Christ is not a slave-owner. Although this word is used in the Pastoral Epistles four times (1 Tim. 6.1, 2; 2 Tim. 2.21; Tit. 2.9), a considerable percentage of the New Testament total of ten, in each case it denotes human slave-owners, but not specifically Christ. Thus the Pauline view on this matter is inconsistent or equivocal, but even so, it is doubtful that Paul's simulation of the Lord Jesus Christ is identical to that of Jude. Also of interest is the letter of James, Jude's purported brother, where *doulos* appears only once, in the first verse: 'James, a servant of God and of the Lord Jesus Christ'. However, James also never uses *despotēs*.

To be sure, the letter of Jude's dramatic master-slave language may be just as heavily connotative as its other striking bits of terminology, but I do not think so. Instead I think that this language tells the reader something quite important about the addressed community, and it does so less vaguely than much of Jude's other language. These people regard these words as non-metaphorical. Although explicit master-slave language does not appear anywhere else in the text of Jude, other passages reinforce this denotative reading of the words 'Master' and 'slave'. Jude 9, a passage that has often mystified readers and that is frequently attributed to the Assumption of Moses, describes the archangel Michael contending with the devil over the body of Moses. Michael says, 'The Lord rebuke you'. On this reading, the Lord Jesus Christ owns the body of his slave Moses, and Michael as Christ's agent does not revile the devil on his own behalf but acts, as himself an obedient slave, only in the Lord's name.

In addition, the fallen angels of Jude 6 are not marked by dalliance with human women but as those who 'did not keep their position' – that is, they did not behave as slaves should. 'Unnatural lust' (or 'going after strange flesh', as the KJV translates the phrase) is mentioned in Jude 7, in connection with Sodom and Gomorrah, but 'defiling the flesh' is elsewhere associated in Jude with disobedience (vv. 8, 23; but see also 12, 13, 15, 16, 18), and not specifically with sexual behavior. This suggests that although Jude's reference to Christ as Master is comparable to that of 2 Peter in important ways, it nevertheless signifies differently on at least one important point: in 2 Peter 'Master' is metaphorically associated with redemption, but in Jude that term is associated with a non-metaphorical demand for obedience.

Since the word *despotēs* appears in close combination with the self-identification of the author as *Iēsou Christou doulos*, the use of *despotēs* in Jude (reinforced by its use in 2 Peter) provides a clue, or at least a highly suggestive contribution, to understanding some of the more metaphorical identifications of Jude's 'licentious, ungodly' ones. These people are compared to the biblical renegades Cain and the followers of Korah (v. 11). Jude says that like 'wild waves ... [or] wandering stars', these 'grumblers [and] malcontents' 'boldly carouse together' (vv. 12-13, 16). In other words, the ungodly ones may or may not deny that Jesus is Christ, but they do deny that Jesus is the only 'Master and Lord'. They may well be Christians, but they deny that Jesus owns them as slaves, and perhaps they even deny that they are anyone's slaves. Jude's claim that they 'look [...] after [*poimainontes*] themselves' (v. 12) further supports the latter understanding (see further Reese 2000: 115-20, but Kelly gives this phrase a narrower reading, 1969: 271). Even more support comes from Jude's descriptions of the ungodly ones as 'following their own passions' (v. 16). This language strongly implies that the ungodly ones, as this name that Jude gives them may also imply (at least, to the author), not only deny that Christ owns them, but they recognize no slave-owner at all. They obey no master but themselves.

By doing this, what these opponents challenge among the beloved is the master-slave structure as a claim upon their obedience (see also Martin 1994: 74). Not only does the letter of Jude not treat slavery to Jesus Christ as a metaphor for redemption, as in 2 Peter, but it seems quite likely that Jude's author would condemn as ungodly anyone who regards 'Master and Lord, Jesus Christ' as a metaphor, even perhaps the author and recipients of 2 Peter. The many modern readers of Jude who see nothing peculiar about its master-slave language follow a tradition that begins, it would seem, with 2 Peter. In this, they are assisted by the translators of these letters (into English, at least), who tone down this language.

To be sure, for the letter of Jude, slavery to Christ *is* salvation, and vice versa. Jude even mentions a 'common salvation' (v. 3), but it appears that the author has decided not to write about that as such, and instead he writes an attack on those who deny 'the faith which was once for all delivered to the saints' (see also v. 20). Jude then argues that 'the grace of God' and the moment when God saved them (vv. 4, 25) came when 'Jesus Christ our Lord' chose the beloved community to be his slaves. The opponents' actions and beliefs subvert this self-understanding of the entire community ('you were once for all fully informed', v. 5) and with it their corresponding belief that they are indeed Christ's slaves. Apparently the ungodly ones have already succeeded in luring some community members away from this faith (vv. 22-23). However, these defections are not merely a threat to the salvation of those individual members, for when the ungodly ones pervert and deny the addressees' faithful commitment to their enslaved status, they threaten the entire community's very well-being as slaves.

This subversive activity would form a major challenge to the 'pastoral power' described in Chapter 1. Even though Jude's author writes as himself a slave of Christ who is addressing other slaves of Christ – for there is only one Master (v. 4) – he does so with authority. Just as Christ is the supreme Shepherd, so Jude's author is a shepherd on behalf of Christ ('to remind you', v. 5; see also v. 17). As Ruth Anne Reese says, the fundamental tension in the letter 'is between the power of the receiver [the beloved community] and the desire of the subject [Jude's author]' (2000: 72), and Elizabeth Castelli notes that 'Foucault reminds us at one point that what is said is not as important as who speaks' (1991: 49).

In other words, signifiers such as 'licentious' or 'ungodly' do not simply reflect some objective meaning, but are themselves given meaning by the one 'who speaks', or in this case, their function within the text (see Nietzsche 1967: 27-31, 36-43). Desjardins argues that the epistle's addressees would be expected to regard their leader as though he were Jesus Christ (1987: 97), and Jeremy Hultin says,

> Jude does what comes naturally: he names one brother, thereby invoking yet another; he displays his knowledge of rare texts and his mastery of interpretation; he writes with rhetorical flourish; he vilifies his opponents, and in all of this he accumulates symbolic capital (2008: 48).

Much as Paul's letters do, but perhaps even more explicitly, the letter of Jude tolerates no threat to pastoral power, and to that end it requires the full participation of the beloved community in the elimination of the ungodly 'blemishes' (v. 12; see also 25). As I noted in Chapter 1, this is Friedrich Nietzsche's 'slave morality' in action. Reese claims that in Jude's letter itself, the infiltrators are not 'functional actors who either cause or undergo an event or events' (2000: 72). Therefore their specific historical or theological identity and even the form of their ungodly licentiousness do not finally matter: the letter's recipients are the important ones, not the opponents. Nevertheless, it is their status that is now profoundly jeopardized by the influence of those opponents, according to Jude.

This contrasts sharply to *Invasion of the Body Snatchers*, where the nature of the pods and their effects on people play an active part in the story. Despite this difference, and much like the character Miles Bennell in that movie, Jude's author urges his fellow slaves of Christ to resist the subversive influence of the infiltrators and to ensure that they remain secure in their slavery (vv. 20-21, 24). Reese comments, speaking of the beloved addressees as 'you' (Jude 2-3, 5, 12, 17-18, 20-21, 24) and the mysterious infiltrators as 'these', terms that Jude repeatedly uses for them (vv. 8, 10-14, 16, 19),

> The narrator ... is responsible for pointing out to the all-knowing 'you' a group of people who have slipped in secretly and whom they have not yet noticed. He is the hero who will announce to the 'you' the threat of the 'these'. Not only does Jude procure for himself a 'saviour' role by rescuing 'you' from their blindness, but he also takes on the role of judge as he points out the error of the 'these' (2000: 68).

Note that if we substitute 'Dr Miles Bennell' for Jude's author, the 'narrator' in Reese's statement, her words become a succinct summary of *Invasion of the Body Snatchers*. Furthermore, the 'you' of that movie becomes not only the characters who populate its narrative world, not unlike the beloved community who are addressed as 'you' so frequently throughout Jude's letter, but also and especially the movie's viewing audience. Bennell's final scream, 'you're next', is addressed directly to the camera and therefore to everyone who watches the movie.

We Know your Little Secret

Like Jude's ungodly ones, the movie's body-snatchers challenge an ideology that is enforced through pastoral power, and its 'you', including the audience, are implicitly the ones who support that ideology and submit to that power. In the film, pastoral power promotes a modern, secular ideology (the small-town 'American way of life', middle-class individualism), but the power itself is arguably directly descended from the ancient Christian mechanism identified by Michel Foucault (Chrulew 2010). It is significant that in the movie, symptoms of the invasion are first noticed by the Santa Mira psychiatrist and the alarm is finally successfully sounded by the town's medical doctor, authorized agents of contemporary pastoral power.

Nocturnal intercourse with nonhuman aliens may even be a modern, secular equivalent to Jude's 'unnatural lust' and 'defiling the flesh' (vv. 7-8, compare Countryman 2006: 749-751, Kelly 1969: 258-259), whether with angels or any other unacceptable partners. This is graphically 'explained' in the 1978 movie, but Jude's letter, like the 1956 film, is more ambiguous, or perhaps simply modest, about 'going after strange flesh'.

More ambiguous language appears in Jude's concluding advice to convince some who doubt, 'save some, by snatching them out of the fire', and to show mercy, even though 'the garment [has been] spotted by the flesh' (vv. 22-23). In light of this joint reading of *Invasion of the Body Snatchers* and the letter of Jude, these phrases cannot refer to the ungodly ones themselves, who after all were 'long ago ... designated for this condemnation', as Jude 4 says. Instead the phrases probably refer to community members who have already been seduced in some way by the infiltrators. Perhaps these people have wavered in their commitment to the Lord Jesus Christ as their only Master, but they have not yet been totally lost to the 'most holy faith' (v. 20, see Kelly 1969: 288-289, Reese 2000: 62, especially n.47). Nevertheless, apart from any such waverers, and as in the movie, for Jude there is no possibility of mediation or conversation between the two committed groups. There can be no mercy or salvation for the body snatchers, or for the ungodly ones.

Both the letter of Jude and Siegel's movie draw upon the tension between what Gilles Deleuze and Félix Guattari call 'schizophrenia' and 'paranoia', in their two volumes subtitled 'Capitalism and Schizophrenia' (1983, 1987). Their distinction, which itself draws upon but also radically rewrites psychoanalytic tradition, does not form an absolute opposition (nor have schizophrenia and paranoia ever been exclusively opposed in psychiatric discourse). Instead, the relation between the two is what Julia Kristeva calls a 'nondisjunction': a 'practically infinite' 'concatenation of deviations' (1980: 40-41). Furthermore, for Deleuze and Guattari, these two terms do not refer simply to the mental abnormalities of individuals, but rather to 'regimes' of desire that govern cultural and social 'machines' of power and signification (see also Deleuze and Guattari 1986: 59-60). Deleuze and Guattari regard the clinical psychoanalytic phenomena of schizophrenia and paranoia as overt but limited instances of these larger cultural and social processes. For them, schizophrenia and paranoia are very much historical, cultural, and political phenomena.

In the schizophrenic machine, inclusive or free disjunctions ('and/or') dissolve all categories and oppositions and generate unrestrained 'desiring-production' (Deleuze and Guattari 1983: 77). In other words, identity and sameness de-construct into multiplicity and difference, and cosmos becomes chaos. The boundaries between self and other tend to disappear.

Even the personal self is 'dismantled' (1987: 151), and the individual ego disintegrates into a 'little group' (1983: 362).

In contrast, in the paranoid machine, the schizophrenic flows of desire are inverted, and the ego as well as the community, along with all of its exclusions and distinctions, are reinforced and organized. Chaos becomes cosmos, and identity-boundaries are tightly drawn. The paranoid machine favors thought and language that universalizes and divides into logical oppositions, including 'biunivocals' such as good versus evil or inside versus outside – or godly versus ungodly. Although it too is a form of desire, paranoia restricts the flows of desire, which are always potentially schizophrenic.

For Deleuze and Guattari, the schizophrenic flows of desiring-production are broken by the 'despotism' (their word) of paranoia, which seeks to master the sign and limit its possible meanings. *Despotēs* always belongs to the signifying realm of paranoia. As they say,

> The paranoid despotic regime: they are attacking me and making me suffer, but I can guess what they're up to, I'm one step ahead of them, I've always known, I have power even in my impotence (1987: 112).

Foucauldian pastoral power is one form of a paranoid despotic regime at work. The paranoid regime seeks to bring the endless unfolding of inclusive or nonrestrictive disjunctions ('wild waves' and 'wandering stars') to a halt, and it does so through a definitive interpretation of signs (which 2 Pet. 1.20-21 makes more explicit than Jude ever does). The paranoid machine shuts down the schizophrenic multiplicity of meaning-possibilities and eliminates the elements of difference, and this in turn culminates in a meaningful world, a Final Signified.

As is very evident in the letter of Jude, paranoia may arise in response to human institutions and events, but ultimately it takes the form of the One God who sees and knows all, who is everywhere and yet invisible, and who demands perfect obedience even as he judges without any chance of appeal. Paranoia is universalizing and monotheistic, and it desires one exclusive truth, such as the single correct Word of God offered by the biblical canon.

It is in this sense of the word 'paranoia' that I call the letter of Jude a paranoid gospel. That the letter actually describes Christ as *despotēs* only makes this explicit. Jude's letter never mentions the word 'gospel' (*euaggelion*), unlike the gospels of Matthew or Mark, or most especially, Paul's letters, where *euaggelion* is a favorite term. However, very much like Paul in Gal. 1.8, which I quoted above, Jude is eager to counter any belief or behavior that might be 'contrary' to 'the faith which was once for all delivered to the saints' (Jude 3), and also to urge the beloved addressees to 'build yourselves up on your most holy faith' (v. 20). Thus while it remains an open question whether or to what extent Jude's author would support Paul's gospel (in striking contrast to 2 Pet. 3.15-16), it seems rather likely that the Pauline concept of the gospel as 'the power of God for salvation to every one who has faith' (Rom. 1.16) would not be a problem for him.

As long as 'the gospel' is defined in this narrowly 'despotic' way, it also seems likely that Jude's author would agree with Paul that there can be only one true gospel – or rather, One True Gospel (see further Chapter 4). That gospel is partly reflected in the letter of Jude, and that part is paranoia. Despite the abundance of connotative tropes in this text, it does not open up plural meanings, but instead it forecloses the schizophrenic multiplicity of possible meanings. Although Reese claims repeatedly that Jude is an 'open' text (2000: 154-155, 165), I think that Jude's text is far from being open or polysemic. (Reese also, and somewhat inconsistently, claims that Jude is 'monologic', 2000: 149.) Jude's many metaphors and other tropes are open to many possible understandings, as all such language is, but their function within that text is consistently and entirely to reinforce, through pastoral power, a paranoid despotic regime in which there is no room for difference. As S.J. Joubert says, Jude's 'syntactic forms and rhetorical strategies ... do not leave any freedom of choice ... to decide whether the presence of the libertinists in their midst are legitimate or not, since the decision has already been made for [the audience]' (1990: 346-347).

Reese also treats the language of Jude as predominantly descriptive and not denunciatory (2000: 143, 164), and she excuses Jude's paranoia (although she does not use that word) as the desire to exercise responsible guardianship over the community. The epistle's language is indeed vividly descriptive, but it is also thoroughly denunciatory, as Joubert's analyses make clear (1990: 341, 343-344; see also Countryman 2007: 751). The reader's only choice is whether to reject utterly the ungodly ones, or to embrace the 'nether gloom ... for ever' or the fire which is the fate of such 'wandering stars' (v. 13; see also vv. 6, 7, 23). It may even be thanks to the unrelenting, denunciatory quality of Jude's descriptions that the modern reader has little clear indication of who the ungodly ones are. The language is brilliant but also vague (as Reese also notes, 2000: 8), leaving the letter available, within the constraints of the master-slave structure, for the use of any Christian group wishing to attack those who are thought to contaminate it, whether they are Jews, pagans, witches, homosexuals, or ethnic or other minorities who might in other circumstances be 'beloved'.

Christopher Frilingos's remark about the book of Revelation is relevant also to Jude: 'A religious disposition was born: Christians believed that the vast resources of the Roman Empire had been mobilized against them ..., that the entire world hated them' (2004: 117-18). The world is divided into 'us' and 'them'. While the Roman Empire only appears indirectly in Jude's exercise of pastoral power – much as Cold War nuclear-arms race fears only appear indirectly in *Invasion of the Body Snatchers* – the sense of insidious, relentless danger is strong. However, this danger does not come from persecution from external forces, as in texts such as 1 Peter, but from a deep sense of contamination that has come from internal sources, and that is therefore less obvious and perhaps all the more pernicious. Like Miles Bennell, Jude's author has an urgent message to deliver, and he 'pulls out all the stops' in his frantic efforts to do so. Each of these 'messages' (the movie and the letter) is consumed by paranoia.

This understanding of Jude suggests an alternative understanding of the movie, in which despite appearances, the pod-people have not been 'possessed' at all. Instead the alien seed pods have 'liberated' these people from some prior state of paranoid enslavement, just as Jude's ungodly ones have freed some of Jude's community from the 'common salvation' that depends upon slavery to – that is, possession by – the 'only Master, Jesus Christ' (vv. 3-4). The pod-people themselves say that the pods do not enslave their human bodies, but instead offer freedom from the all-too-human cares and life that had formerly oppressed them. Prior to its invasion, Santa Mira is apparently inhabited entirely by uniformly pleasant, well-educated people, as are many small towns in 1950s movies and TV shows. The Santa Mirans are 'possessed' by the paranoia of their thoroughly middle-class life-styles just as surely as the faithful Christians of Jude's beloved community are possessed by Christ. The movie's townspeople are the (godly) ones who support and submit to a powerful ideology, and the movie's 'you', the viewing audience to whom Miles screams, are also implicitly supporters of that same bourgeois ideology and submit to that same pastoral power. It is the body-snatchers who correspond to the ungodly ones and who challenge that ideology.

Dr Bennell is a charming, flesh-and-blood human being, unlike 'Jude ... [the] brother of James', who never emerges from the shadows, and the detailed specificity of the movie's fictional Santa Mira contrasts sharply to the vagueness of the letter's beloved community. Despite these differences, the homogeneity of the pleasant little town seems very much like that of Jude's addressees, the faithful, undivided (v. 19) slaves of Christ. This returns us to the disputed understanding of the film as an allegory of 1950s anti-Communist hysteria, to which we might add anti-beatnik (it was too early then for the hippies), anti-feminist, and anti-'colored' fears that were also widespread even if not as often overtly expressed in middle-class white America at that time. The monochrome film of Siegel's movie is especially appropriate for such a 'black-and-white' world. The letter of Jude also presents a black-and-white world. Like the pod-people of that film, Jude's ungodly ones have apparently broken free from their 'possession' by Christ, and as the letter says, the consequence is something like madness, for they have become 'wild waves [and] wandering stars' (v. 13).

UR NXT

In today's world of email and text messaging, we have become used to replacing words or short phrases by initials or other sorts of alphabetic shorthand. FWIW, ROTFL, TTFN. Perhaps the ancient Christians started the practice with their *nomina sacra* abbreviations, or perhaps the practice of abbreviating frequently used or specially familiar words is as old as writing itself. Abbreviation seems to be intrinsic to any writing. In the last few years, several of my friends and I have begun to abbreviate 'biblical studies' as 'bs' in our emails, and this has led us to abbreviate 'biblical scholar' as 'bs-er'. Not the most respectful abbreviations, I'm afraid, but also not completely inappropriate. As I was writing this chapter, I realized that the phrase, 'body snatcher', could also be abbreviated as 'bs-er', and as I thought about that, I realized that this silly coincidence illuminates a possible contemporary understanding of the letter of Jude.

Biblical scholars are sometimes regarded by others – their students, especially, but also church laity, the general public, and even scholars in other fields – not as heartless monsters from outer space, I hope, but nonetheless as ungodly persons who pervert the grace of God and deny the Lord Jesus Christ, especially if they teach about the Bible's texts in a critical and not always devout manner. All you need to do is search the Internet for online discussions of, for example, the authenticity of the letters of Jude or 2 Peter, to find examples of readers saying very harsh things about many of the books cited in this one. In the eyes of many devout Christians, biblical scholars revile the glorious ones in their scholarly writings and in their teaching, and thereby they deserve the punishment that Jude proclaims for the rebellious angels and the followers of Korah – that is, to be consigned to the nether darkness forever. People say to them – and I of course am one of 'them' – much as Becky Driscoll says to Miles Bennell as they flee from the pod-people, 'I don't want a world without love or grief or beauty'. Biblical scholars are perceived as turning the Bible into a cold, soul-less thing, without love or grief or beauty.

Biblical scholars may not be body snatchers, but we are Bible snatchers. We are infiltrators among the godly ones. Despite this, as Desjardins notes, the common scholarly approach to the letter of Jude is to assume that the author and his beloved community are the 'good guys', who will eventually be known as more or less orthodox Christians, and that the infiltrators must then be the 'bad guys', heretics for sure and if not gnostics, then something else just as bad, much like modern skeptics (1987: 92). In other words, the scholars themselves, by and large and regardless of (but often because of) their own personal beliefs, do not identify with the ungodly ones of Jude's letter, but rather with the beloved Christian community, and with Jude's author.

Nevertheless, there are some biblical scholars who choose to read the Bible outside of the historical and theological parameters as approved by even the mainstream Christian or at least scholarly majority. These scholars read the biblical books as Martians, as I said in the Preface. They would surely appear to the author and to the first recipients of the letter of Jude as alien monsters, or at the very least as waterless clouds and fruitless trees, loud-mouthed boasters who follow only their own passions and cast aside all respectability. This smaller group – and I confess to being one of 'them' as well – may not exactly be unhuman pod-people, but they do sometimes question the value of 'humanity' in an increasingly posthuman world (see Hayles 1999). Perhaps that is even worse. Would the author of Jude have approved of a book such as this one? Probably not.

Invasion of the Body Snatchers and the letter of Jude illuminate one another, even as they cast intertextual light on 'paranoid despotic regimes'. In our own history, we have repeatedly seen the horrors that result from beliefs in communal uniformity and One True Church, and the misery caused by ethnic cleansing and religious zealotry. No matter how well justified it may be, any paranoia is always worse than that which it would eradicate. Thus maybe it is the bs-ers who are the good guys after all. Perhaps if our fear of body snatchers or ungodly ones turns us into people who cannot abide difference, then it would be better if we became pod-people or wandering stars.

3

Taming Paranoia: 2 Peter Rewrites Jude

[I]n order to transform a work into a cult object one must be able to break, dislocate, unhinge it so that one can remember only parts of it, irrespective of their original relationship with the whole (Eco 1986: 198).

[I]t is a mistake to regard the heresies in both epistles [of Jude and 2 Peter] as in all respects coincident (Kelly 1969: 355).

Creative Rewriting

In this chapter, I examine the biblical letter of 2 Peter as though it were a rewriting of the letter of Jude. In doing so, I may be failing to read as a Martian would (and as I proposed to do in the Preface), but then, I am not a Martian, only an Earthling who is trying to read as one. Nevertheless, it is my hope that in this way I can uncover and explore points at which my efforts to read in this way have failed – and more important, significant differences between these two texts.

Terrance Callan observes that '2 Peter has thoroughly reworked Jude to serve its own purposes', and he claims that this gave 'new meaning to the Jude material' (2004: 64, 63). While many others have examined the differences and similarities between the two letters, the prevailing tendency has been, as Callan indicates, to uncover the 'purposes' of 2 Peter in its 'use' of Jude. In contrast, my interest is not to uncover the purposes of 2 Peter, whatever they might be, or any historical features of that letter. Instead I consider 2 Peter as a rewriting of Jude in order to examine the meaning-potentialities of each text in relation to the other, as afterlife and precursor. The reworking of Jude in 2 Peter results in significant tensions between the two texts, not unlike translation tensions between a 'target' text and its 'source' text.

In translations, according to Walter Benjamin, 'The life of the originals attains ... to its ever-renewed latest and most abundant flowering' (1968: 72). Translation is a kind of resurrection. Each source text lives on in another text which enables it to 'speak' again, perhaps in new or even very different ways (that is, a new language), even as the translated, target text threatens to silence its precursor utterly – that is, to replace it – which sometimes happens. Much the same thing happens when a text is rewritten. Like a translation, the rewriting of any text 'creates' its source text as an 'original' (Benjamin 1968: 81). Prior to that rewriting, whatever the source text was, it was not the original basis of another text. In that sense, it was not a 'source'. After it has been rewritten, it may disappear altogether, or at least 'lose' any significant difference from its rewritten afterlife.

Although neither translation nor rewriting does anything to the source text's physical signifiers, nevertheless that text's significance changes once it has been translated or rewritten, for it has become among other things the source of another text, and it has thereby changed into something that it had not been before. The signifiers have not changed, but they signify differently. This holds true regardless of whether that text is a story, a song, or in the present case, a letter.

The history of literature is filled with such rewritings, which transform their source texts in many different ways and in so doing take on themselves a variety of different forms. Just like translations, rewritings may be more or less 'literal' or 'free'. James Joyce's great novel, *Ulysses* (1986), follows Homer's classic epic, *The Odyssey* (Lattimore 1967), on a roughly episode-by-episode basis, but it freely transforms the sorrows and triumphs of the 'god-like' hero Odysseus, on his homeward journey after a long absence and many trials, into a single day in the life of a modest advertising salesman, Leopold Bloom, as he wanders around the city of Dublin. Each of these texts tells a great story in its own right, but the reader who is familiar with both of them is almost inevitably drawn back and forth between them as the two narratives continually illuminate one another.

A different sort of rewriting appears in several of the very short writings of Franz Kafka. Kafka rewrites various narratives from antiquity, including stories from the *Odyssey* as well as biblical stories of the tower of Babel, Abraham, and Mount Sinai. In the tiny story, 'The Building of the Temple', the familiar account from 1 Kings 6 reappears, more exaggerated and even more dream-like than in the source text. However, after describing the temple's seemingly effortless construction, the story announces that

> instruments obviously of a magnificent sharpness had been used to scratch on every stone ... for an eternity outlasting the temple, the clumsy scribblings of senseless children's hands, or rather the entries of barbaric mountain dwellers (1958: 47).

Not unlike both of the letters of Jude and 2 Peter, Kafka's story suggests that there are 'blemishes' on the holy edifice (see Kelly 1969: 185). However, very much unlike the desire expressed or at least implied in those two letters, the stain or blot in Kafka's story will never go away.

Perhaps closer still to the subject matter of this chapter is Jorge Luis Borges's story, 'Pierre Menard, Author of Don Quixote' (1962: 45-55). Borges's story is not itself a rewriting of another text, but rather it describes the imaginary rewriting of an actual text, *Don Quixote*, by a fictional character. Pierre Menard, a twentieth-century Frenchman, decides to write a book that will coincide, chapter for chapter and even word for word and letter for letter, with the famous novel by the seventeenth-century Spaniard, Miguel de Cervantes. This rewriting will yield an *exactly identical* story. According to Borges's story, Menard did not finish his task, and the reader is told that all that he completed was two chapters and part of a third. The nameless narrator then compares the text produced by Menard to that of Cervantes:

> the fragmentary *Don Quixote* of Menard is more subtle than that of Cervantes. The latter indulges in a rather coarse opposition between tales of knighthood and the meager, provincial reality of his country; Menard chooses as 'reality' the land of Carmen during the century of Lepanto and Lope. ... The text of Cervantes and that of Menard are verbally identical, but the second is almost infinitely richer (1962: 51-52).

Borges's story satirizes a whole complex of modern literary assumptions: the value of authorial intention and the social context in which the text is written, the importance of the 'original' text in interpretation, and the function of influence and imitation in literary history. It also supports my point that any rewriting of a text, no matter how literal or free (or imaginary), will never be 'the same' as its source text. Even though Menard's text is not a translation, still the 'ever-renewed latest and most abundant flowering' of the text that Benjamin describes in a literal translation is evident in it. Although his 'translation' of Cervantes's novel is perfectly 'literal', it evidently does not mean 'the same thing' as the source, not only because it was produced in a different time and place, but also simply because it is the afterlife.

My goal is to examine the ways that the much longer letter of 2 Peter 'corrects' or elaborates on the letter of Jude. The reasons for thinking that 2 Peter is a rewriting of Jude were explained in Chapter 1, but even though that argument is very strong, like any historical argument it can lead only to a more or less probable conclusion. In the following, I accept this concept as a working hypothesis, a historical fiction presupposed for this comparative reading of the two letters, and nothing more. The differences that appear between the texts are understood to be changes, alterations of the signifiers that result in altered meaning possibilities. Understood in this way, these changes imply things about each of the texts – that is, not only how 2 Peter appropriates Jude but also how Jude remains distinct from 2 Peter (not unlike *The Odyssey* and *Ulysses*) – apart from any question of which one came first. I make no claim whether these changes are improvements or not.

Although 2 Peter makes a great deal of sense as an expansion or correction of Jude, the 'sense' that appears when the two letters are read together must also be examined closely and critically. This sense grounds a sort of canonical effect. Indeed, by rewriting Jude as it did, 2 Peter may have in effect helped Jude (and thereby also itself) to get into the New Testament canon. I will say more about this in Chapter 4. In any case, the inclusion of both a source text and its target text within the single unity of the biblical canon itself signifies something – something more than the sum of the two texts.

In order to manage my analysis, I divide 2 Peter into three parts, which correspond to the three chapters of this letter. The first chapter of 2 Peter can be treated as a single unit mainly because 2.1 is where the first clear rewriting of Jude appears. Prior to that point, there are elements in 2 Peter that bear comparison to Jude, but no strong evidence of rewriting. Nevertheless, the first chapter of 2 Peter flows without literary break into the second chapter, in which the rewriting of Jude dominates the text, and the material in the first chapter is not unrelated to this later material. Finally, 2 Peter's third chapter, while not drawing as strongly on the letter of Jude as the second chapter does, continues to do so in important ways. However, this chapter is also where the greatest disparity between the two letters opens up. As a result, a continuous comparison between the two letters almost constantly illuminates each of them.

Second Peter's First Chapter

The openings of both letters (Jude 1-2 and 2 Pet. 1.1-2) closely follow well-known conventions of the Hellenistic epistle: identification of the writer, address to the recipients, and greeting. However, already there appears a tension between 2 Peter's unequivocal identification of its writer as 'apostle of Jesus Christ' and Jude's more ambiguous 'brother of James', especially since claims to apostolic authority often counted heavily in early Christianity. Even assuming that Jude's James is the well-known brother of Jesus and early leader of the Jerusalem church (see Chapter 1), Jude's language requires from the reader a series of inferences that 2 Peter does not. It is as though Jude is playing a little guessing game with the reader, and 2 Peter is not. Thus 2 Peter's claim to importance and authority is already less troubled and uncertain than is that of Jude.

Similarly, the addressees in Jude are merely 'those who are called, beloved … and kept', but the addressees in 2 Peter are 'those who have obtained a faith of equal standing with ours'. To be called, beloved, and kept is well enough, but it is hardly the same as having faith equal to that of the apostle Peter. Second Peter's apparent replacement of Jude's 'mercy' and 'love' with 'grace' and 'knowledge' may also be significant, especially given the later importance of *agapē* (love) in Jude 12 and especially *(epi)gnōsis* (knowledge) in 2 Pet. 1.3, 5, 6, 8, 2.20, and 3.18. It is Jude's narrator who is urgent (*spoudēn*, 'eager') to write to the beloved community in v. 3, but in 2 Pet. 1.5 it is the community who should be urgent (*spoudēn*, 'make ... effort') to strengthen their faith (see also 1.10 and 3.14, 'be ... zealous'). A consistent shift already appears in the direction of a stronger sense of identity and communal solidarity (or 'stability', 3.17; see also 1.6, 3.16) in 2 Peter.

This emphasis is developed further in the next several verses of 2 Peter, 1.3-11, which in the Greek text flow directly from 1.2 and are not comparable to Jude. In this section, 2 Peter exercises 'pastoral power' (see Chapter 1) within the community, repeating several times the importance of knowledge and also introducing the theme of 'godliness', which plays an important part in both 2 Peter and in Jude, both directly and through its opposition to the corruptions of that which is 'ungodly'. Second Peter speaks of both the godly (*eusebēs*) and the ungodly (*asebēs*), but Jude restricts its language to the ungodly only. For 2 Peter, the 'divine power' and 'promises' of Jesus Christ, or possibly God (1.3-4), offer hope that the believers may 'become partakers of the divine nature', although whether this implies mysticism or even pantheism is disputed among the scholars. Nothing like this appears in Jude.

According to 2 Peter, the orderly sequence of qualities which believers should acquire (1.5-7) presents a clear means through which they can avoid the 'corruption' and 'defilements of the world' (2.19-20) and live 'lives of holiness and godliness' (3.11), culminating in 'entrance into the eternal kingdom of our Lord and Savior Jesus Christ' (1.11). Jude does not mention any kingdom, whether of God or of Christ. The Christians addressed in 2 Peter have control over themselves and their lives, as 1.6 states explicitly, and they are effective and fruitful (1.8). 'You will never fall' in 2 Pet. 1.10 echoes but also shifts the focus of 'keep you from falling' in Jude 24.

This section in 2 Peter not only further clarifies the letter's opening but identifies those 'things' (1.3, 8-9) of which its community is reminded in 1.12, 'though you know them and are established in the truth'. Although this language echoes Jude's 'desire to remind you, though you were once for all fully informed' (v. 5), in contrast to 2 Peter, Jude's remark seems petulant and introduces a rather disorderly sequence of comments on scriptural texts (including *1 Enoch*), instead of concluding an orderly discussion of the Christian's 'things' as in 2 Peter. In contrast to Jude, 2 Peter's own sequence of scripture citations is both exclusively 'canonical' (no explicit reference to Enoch or the story of Michael and the devil, as in Jude) and also follows the Torah sequence, unlike Jude (see Leaney 1967: 78). However, 2 Peter's more orderly sequence of comments on the scriptures will not commence until its second chapter, when the rewriting of Jude begins in earnest.

Second Peter 1.13-21 also has little that is comparable to Jude. It opens with a continuation of the theme of reminding (begun in 1.12 and repeated in 1.15), conjoined to remarks suggesting that the aged apostle Peter is now approaching his death, apparently alluding to Jesus' prediction at the end of the gospel of John (21.18-19). The letter's reference to itself in 2 Pet. 1.15 is intriguing, and suggests a very different sort of literature (see Aichele 2006: 31-58), but as J.N.D. Kelly notes in another vein, 'it savours of an epoch when the living witness of the apostles is no longer operative and the Church feels the need of written texts stamped with their authority' (1969: 315). In this verse the letter comes close to identifying itself as 'scripture'.

Although much of the previous material anticipates 2 Peter's arguments to come, the first serious hint of the troublemakers appears in 1.16, where 'cleverly devised myths' are abjured in favor of the coming of Jesus Christ, whose 'majesty' has allegedly already been witnessed directly by the writer. Perhaps the reference to myths coheres with 2 Peter's rejection of 'one's own interpretation' in the matter of 'prophecy of scripture' (1.20), as both clever myths and personal interpretation might imply excessive freedom of imagination or desire. Since interpretation of the Jewish scriptures figures prominently in 2 Peter, the implied author assures the reader in advance that his comments on the scriptures do not consist of cleverly devised myths or his own interpretations but come instead from someone 'moved by the Holy Spirit' (1.21).

Nevertheless, that (true) prophecy must come from the Holy Spirit also hints at a deep distrust of written texts, which is not explicitly stated in this letter (unlike 2 Cor. 3.6: 'the written code kills, but the Spirit gives life'). This distrust would stand in some tension with 2 Peter's apparently high valuation of 'the scriptures', including the writings of Paul (see 3.15-16). Although the allusions to Peter's foretold death as well as his witnessing of something like the transfiguration of Jesus (1.14, 16) do not necessarily imply that the letter's author or recipients are familiar with some form of the gospels of John and perhaps Matthew (see Chapter 1), that would not be impossible if the letter were written in the later first or second century. Second Peter's language suggests that the scriptures are necessary but potentially dangerous, because they require interpretation, and the letter's own interpretations of the scriptures are evidently exercises in controlling the dangerous writings and inviting the imitation described in Chapter 1. Neither the opponents' stories (*muthois*) nor their interpretations of scripture are acceptable, and the desire reflected in 2 Peter to control the selection of stories and the generation of interpretations is already heading in the direction of demand for a canon (see further below).

The letter of Jude mentions and interprets numerous texts from the Jewish scriptures and apocrypha, but it does not explicitly mention 'the scriptures' or their interpretation, or 'myths'. In addition, Jude makes no acknowledgment of any Christian scriptures, except perhaps the quotation in v. 18, which does not match any ancient text except 2 Pet. 3.3, which presumably rewrites Jude. Nevertheless, similar statements may be found in Acts 20.29-30 and 1 Tim. 4.1-2. However, Jude's concern for 'our common salvation' and 'the faith which was once for all delivered to the saints' (v. 3), as opposed to the 'loud-mouthed boasting' of those who 'deny our only Master and Lord' (vv. 4, 16) also hints at a desire to control that community's beliefs which is not unlike 2 Peter's desire to control stories and interpretation.

Callan (2006: 145) suggests that 2 Peter's metaphoric description of the prophetic word as 'a lamp shining in a dark place, until the day dawns and the morning star rises' (1.19) implies that the addressees believe that the world is a dark place of corruption and defilement (see 2.19-20, compare Jn 1.5). This may be also suggested by the phrase that follows, 'in your hearts', but that would imply that this dawning of the day is also (like the lamp) a metaphor, perhaps for understanding or faith, and not a reference to a forthcoming event. However, 2 Peter later asserts that the world will be replaced by 'new heavens and a new earth in which righteousness dwells' (3.13), and this is described as the 'day of God' (3.12, see 3.10). The impression given throughout 2 Peter 3 is that this event will be more than merely personal or psychological (see Callan 2006: 148). This may be why 2 Pet. 1.20 cautions against 'one's own interpretation' and the 'impulse of man'.

Yet this verse also opens up a can of worms, for the problem of distinguishing between simple human desire and the influence of the divine spirit appears again and again in the Jewish and Christian scriptures and vexes every attempt at interpretation – including any interpretations of 2 Peter itself. Kelly argues that 1.20-21 implies an assertion of apostolic authority against opponents who believe that all prophets speak only their own impulses (1969: 324-325), and while this may be consistent with the idea that the opponents are influenced by some skeptical Hellenistic philosophy (see below), that conclusion also requires the reader to do quite a lot of 'interpreting' of this text.

Second Peter's Second Chapter

There is no significant break between the first two chapters of 2 Peter, since 2.1 continues the theme of prophecy and interpretation that was introduced in 1.19-21. However, chap. 2 is where 2 Peter's rewriting of Jude is most strongly apparent, and the seeds of paranoia that were planted in chap. 1, with words such as 'corruption' and 'passion' (1.4) and phrases such as 'cleverly devised myths' (1.16), begin to blossom, most immediately in the secrecy associated with the infiltrators. These ungodly ones will be either condemned (Jude 4) or destroyed (2 Pet. 2.1). The phrase, 'swift destruction', is not in Jude, and it also supports 2 Peter's greater apocalyptic tendencies. In Jude the opponents 'pervert the grace of our God' by denying Jesus Christ as Master, while in 2 Peter they will bring in 'destructive heresies'. The shift in meaning is small, but as I noted in Chapter 1, 2 Peter leans more than Jude does toward concern with doctrine rather than behavior. Perhaps this is why 'knowledge' is of such great interest in that letter.

In 2 Pet. 2.1, 'the Master who bought them' implies that the addressed community regard themselves as slaves who have been bought by Jesus Christ, the Master, from some other owner, perhaps 'corruption' or, more generally, 'the world' (2.19, 20). Whether the addressees believe that Christ bought only them or that he is everyone's Master is not clear, but 2.1 makes it clear that the heresy of the 'false teachers' includes denial that Christ is their Master (see Callan 2001b: 549-550). As I noted in Chapter 1, 'Master' (*despotēs*) occurs in the New Testament only here and in Jude 4 to refer to Jesus Christ as a slave owner.

Elsewhere in the New Testament, either *despotēs* is used of ordinary human slave-owners or else the word connotes God, not Christ. In each of these latter cases, Lk. 2.29, Acts 4.24, and Rev. 6.10, *despotēs* appears in a prayer addressed to God, where the word is translated by the Revised Standard Version as 'Lord' or 'Sovereign Lord'. In the other instances (1 Tim. 6.1, 2; 2 Tim. 2.21; Tit. 2.9; 1 Pet. 2.18), where the word more clearly denotes human slave-owners, the RSV translates this word as 'master' (with lower-case 'm'). A differential translation practice appears to be in effect, similar to the translation of the corresponding word, *doulos* (slave, servant, see Chapter 2), and probably driven by theology. Because both Jude and 2 Peter distinguish between Jesus Christ and God (see Chapter 1), it is unlikely in either text that the term 'Master' is being used of Jesus as though he were God, or even as God's representative. As A.R.C. Leaney says, 'in these Letters *our Lord* or 'Master' means Christ and not God the Father' (1967: 136, his emphasis; see also Kelly 1969: 327).

I argued in Chapter 2 that a non-metaphoric understanding of Christ as slave-owner and thus of the Christian as his slave plays a significant role in Jude's struggle between the beloved community and the ungodly ones. The letter of Jude's richly connotative language promotes slippage and multiplicity of meanings, and as a result, a definitive 'solution' to the hermeneutic question of: 'Who are the ungodly ones?' cannot be found. Nevertheless, it does appear that Jude's ungodly ones recognize no master at all, as they are chaotic and disorderly: they are the true anti-nomians or even better, an-archists, like wild waves or wandering stars (v. 13).

In contrast, 2 Peter's unrighteous ones are still slaves, for they are 'slaves of corruption' (2.19). Although they are similar to the ungodly ones of Jude, having denied 'the Master who bought them', nevertheless they have accepted another master in his place. They still follow a law, albeit an other (heretical) law. In other words, for 2 Peter, there is no freedom 'option': you must be a slave to one master or another. However, this exclusivity is enriched by the likelihood that 'Master' has metaphorical meaning in 2 Peter, which is evident in the soteriological connotations of the phrase 'who bought them', and also in the words, 'the eternal kingdom of our Lord and Savior Jesus Christ' (1.11), as well perhaps as 2 Peter's use of the important word *parousia* (see further below).

Here 2 Peter may be compared to 1 Pet. 2.16, according to which Christians should live 'as free men' but also 'as servants [*douloi*] of God'. Furthermore, 'slaves of corruption' is also evidently a metaphor, and given the strong apocalyptic tendencies of 2 Peter, one suspects that this entire metaphoric structure of masters and slaves is another expression of that apocalypticism. In other words, to live as though 'the Master has bought you' is 'to be found without spot or blemish' and thereby gain entry 'into the eternal kingdom' of 'new heavens and a new earth'.

If the metaphorical quality of 'Master' and 'slave' in 2 Peter were merely 'as though', then 2 Peter's view on the matter would be quite far from Jude's, despite the similarity of language. However, not all metaphors are simply vivid comparisons. If I describe my friend as 'a peach', you will not (I hope) think that she is a delicious fruit, but if I describe my friend as 'a hero', then you should think that she really has heroic qualities. I think that this master-slave language should be taken as reflecting serious beliefs – not necessarily the beliefs of the people involved, but how these letters depict those beliefs. In 2 Peter as in Jude, the addressed community believes that they really are Christ's slaves, but in 2 Peter they also believe that this means something more.

Although Christ is regularly described as Savior in 2 Peter (1.1, 11, 2.20, 3.2, 18; see also 3.15) and elsewhere in the New Testament (for example, Lk. 2.11), he is not ever so described in the letter of Jude. In Jude 25, it is God who is the savior 'through Jesus Christ'. In other words, in Jude Jesus may be said to 'save' the Christian only in the sense that he owns her as a slave. Phrases such as 'unto eternal life' and 'before the presence of his glory' (vv. 21, 24) may well connote some concept of salvation, but Jude develops no further context for them. By using *despotēs* as a metaphor for redemption – the word does not change, but the meaning shifts, as in Borges's story about Pierre Menard – 2 Peter 'masters' Jude's unruly language and produces instead clarity and order.

Considered as a rewriting of Jude's letter, 2 Peter clarifies and explains the other text's abrupt introduction of the concept of Christ as Master, which comes in that text for all practical purposes at its very beginning. By more carefully building up through an orderly series of transitions through chap. 1, 2 Peter eliminates Jude's abruptness and considerably reduces its frantic tone. Second Pet. 2.1 identifies the opponents as false teachers and heretics, and the next two verses further expand upon, revise, or clarify Jude's language ('licentious', 'revile', 'way of Cain', 'flattering', 'gain advantage'). As before, 2 Peter's tendency to expand and clarify what is vague in Jude results in greater control over the possibilities for meaning, and thus less confusion for the reader. Kelly argues that 2 Pet. 2.2-3 refers to the entire Christian 'way of life' (1969: 328), but that is not explicitly stated. In addition, while it may be true that the opponents really are greedy and exploit the community, this may again be 'loaded language' that reflects the seriousness of hostility and disagreement between the letter's author and the opponents, or even a purely rhetorical move, but nothing more.

The remainder of the second chapter of 2 Peter, 2.4-22, is given over to a rewriting of Jude 5-16, which is rearranged, often expanded and elaborated, and occasionally reduced. As might be expected from the foregoing, the general tendency of these changes is to make 2 Peter both more reader-friendly and less inflammatory than Jude's letter. Callan argues that 'In this way the author of 2 Peter transformed Jude's list of precedents for punishment of sinners and critique of its opponents into a refutation of the false teachers' denial of a final judgment' (2004: 49). Second Peter's 'prophecies of scripture' have been arranged into proper canonical sequence, with additional insertions of examples of God's grace to the righteous: Noah and the flood (2.5), and Lot (2.7, by way of contrast to Sodom and Gomorrah, which is mentioned in Jude 7). The exodus from Egypt is omitted, as are Cain and Korah. Additional comments on the biblical stories make the point clearer. 'Accursed children' in 2 Pet. 2.14 echoes Isa. 57.4, but out of canonical sequence.

The explicit *1 Enoch* reference in Jude 14-15 does not appear in 2 Peter's survey of the scriptures, but the understanding of the fate of the rebel angels as found in Jude 6 is elaborated by reference to 'hell' (the Hellenistic Tartaros, 2.4). In addition, Jude's story of Michael disputing with the devil is rewritten to remove any specific allusion to the Assumption of Moses (2.10-11). Kelly suggests that 2 Peter, unlike Jude, does not regard the Jewish apocryphal texts as scripture (1969: 331, 338). However, the allusion to *1 Enoch* remains in 2.4, and Jerome Neyrey notes similarities between 2 Pet. 2.4-9 and LXX Sirach 16.6-23 (1980: 427-28), another apocryphal text. Some of Jude's non-scriptural metaphors for the ungodly ones ('irrational animals ... instinct', 'blemishes', 'waterless clouds/springs ... winds/ storm') appear again in 2 Peter, although they are sometimes modified, and others are added ('eyes full of adultery', 'slaves of corruption'). A few of

Jude's more striking metaphors are omitted ('fruitless trees', 'wild waves', 'wandering stars').

'Cast into hell' (*tartarōsas*, 2.4) is unique to 2 Peter in the New Testament, but there may be a pun on or echo of this Greek word in the word 'kept [*tēreō*, reserved]' in relation to the 'nether gloom of darkness', which appears in Jude 6, 13, and 2 Pet. 2.9, 17, 3.7, and by way of contrast, 'kept for Jesus Christ' or 'in the love of God' in Jude 1 and 21. Both the unrighteous and the righteous are 'kept' in Jude, but in different places or states, whereas only the unrighteous are 'kept' in 2 Peter. This change would correlate to their differing uses of master-slave language.

Second Peter repeatedly emphasizes that God rescues the righteous (2.5, 7, 9), a theme that does not appear at all in the corresponding material in Jude. Perhaps Jude's use of *tēreō* in relation to both the righteous and unrighteous was unacceptable to 2 Peter's author, and as a result the 'keeping' of the righteous was replaced by their 'rescue' (salvation) at these points in the letter. According to 2 Pet. 2.5, Noah's flood was a catastrophe of cosmic proportions, and in that respect not unlike an apocalyptic cataclysm in which many are destroyed and a few are saved. Similarly, as Callan says, 2 Pet. 2.6-8

> seems to see Lot as a type of his readers. Just as Lot was saved from Sodom and Gomorrah when they were destroyed by fire, the readers will be saved when the present heavens and earth are destroyed by fire. Like them, Lot was a just man living among those engaged in licentiousness and lawless deeds (2001b: 555).

Unlike Leaney (1967: 122), Kelly separates 2 Pet. 2.10 into two halves, and he notes that 2.10a is very close to some of the language in Jude 7-8 (1969: 335-36). In this way, these texts both connect sexual misbehavior to rejection by the Lord, who is the 'authority [*kuriotēs*, from *kurios*]'. Betsy Bauman-Martin notes that several of Jude's scriptural references which appear also in 2 Peter allude to stories of improper mixings, not only between humans, but between human and divine beings, and their hybrid consequences (2008: 69-71). In L. William Countryman's reading of Jude, sexual encounters with angels on the part of the opponents, in 'dreams' and leading to 'unnatural' ejaculations (connoted in Jude 8, 13), are precisely the evil to which Jude is pointing (2007: 749-51; see also Martin 1994: 69). One wonders what Jude's community would make of the Gospel of Luke's story of divine–human interbreeding and the resulting 'strange flesh' (Jude 7, KJV), which echoes many pagan Hellenistic stories. If the communities addressed by Jude and 2 Peter clearly distinguish between God and Jesus Christ, as Leaney suggests (1967: 88, 139), then perhaps the opponents that Jude at least finds revolting are not heretics at all by orthodox standards, but instead the sort of Christians who would approve of Luke–Acts and its hybrid, divine–human messiah.

Kelly rejects any connection between 2 Pet. 2.10a and 2.10b, and he calls 2.10b-22 'the most violent and colourfully expressed tirade in the NT' (1969: 337). Galatians 5.12 is surely as ferocious, although briefer, and passages from the Revelation of John might also be contenders for this award, but this passage would certainly offer serious competition. According to Callan, in 2 Pet. 2.10b-22, 'the author reworked a portion of Jude that attempted to prove Jude's thesis into a digression in which the author of 2 Peter denounced his opponents' (2003: 57). Nevertheless, despite all the violence and color, even here Jude's language, when it appears, tends to be toned down.

Kelly cites *1 Enoch* and concludes that the 'glorious ones' of 2.10b (but not necessarily Jude 8, even though the same wording appears there) are the fallen angels mentioned in Jude 6 and 2 Pet. 2.4 (1969: 338; see 263-64). In contrast, Leaney seems to think that the 'glorious ones' in both Jude and 2 Peter might be any angels (1967: 122; see 90). According to Kelly's division of 2 Pet. 2.10, although the phrase, 'irrational animals', in Jude 10 may refer to the opponents' 'unnatural lust' and reviling of the glorious ones (vv. 7-9), in 2 Pet. 2.12 the same words refer instead to the opponents' ignorance and presumption concerning the glorious ones. Again there is a shift in focus from improper behavior in Jude to false doctrine in 2 Peter.

Second Pet. 2.13 provides one of the more complex (and explicit) instances of rewriting Jude. Indeed, anyone still wishing to argue that Jude rewrote 2 Peter would encounter serious difficulties at this point. The initial phrase in the RSV translation of this verse concludes the comment in 2.12 about irrational animals (see above). This is followed in Greek by two participial phrases which are often translated as two separate sentences. The New English Bible substantially rewrites the entire passage. The first phrase may continue the thought about irrational animals, as the King James Version suggests, in contrast to the RSV and New Revised Standard Version.

The second phrase, 'They are blots and blemishes, reveling in their dissipation, carousing with you' (RSV), seems to transform Jude 12. Jude's community shares 'love feasts', and the exact phrase used to refer to these events in v. 12, *agapais ... suneuōchoumenoi*, appears also in several of the oldest manuscripts of 2 Pet. 2.13. Apart from these two texts, *suneuōcheomai* ('carouse with') appears nowhere else in the New Testament. According to Kelly, Jude 12 is the earliest use of *agapē* to refer to Christian communal meals: 'suppers, religious in character and representing a primitive Christian adaptation of Jewish practice' (1969: 269; see also Martin 1994: 70). Apparently these meals were initially linked among Christians with the sacrament of eucharist (*eucharistia*, 'thanksgiving'), but later they were treated as separate occasions.

However, in other manuscripts of 2 Peter, the very similar phrase *apatais ...suneuōchoumenoi* appears instead at 2.13, and this phrase is translated in the RSV as 'dissipation' (also NRSV; KJV has 'deceivings'; NEB has 'deceptions'). So translated, this phrase seems to connect with the 'daytime revel' mentioned just previously in 2.13. According to Kelly, 'this latter reading can scarcely be original' (1969: 341). Further complicating things, *apatē* ('deceptive') also appears instead of *agapē* ('love') at Jude 12 in a few manuscripts; apparently ancient scribes were trying to set things right, 'correcting' the text, but in opposite 'directions'. Leaney suggests that the phrase in 2 Peter should be understood as 'mock love-feasts' (1967: 122-123). Other interpretations of this language are listed by Callan (2003: 56).

As I noted in Chapter 1, most scholars (including translators) treat the texts of these letters as though the opponents are in the wrong. They also tend to regard both letters' groups of 'good guys' as more or less orthodox, and therefore sharing similar beliefs and practices. A quite different possibility would be that 2 Peter is mocking 'love feasts' such as those of the Jude community, which are promoted by the opponents in the 2 Peter community. In other words, the author of 2 Peter finds the love feasts of proto-orthodox Christianity, including Jude's community, distasteful. The letter of 2 Peter attributes these feasts to the opponents and says nothing at all about any feasts held by the faithful community, although the text implies that the opponents' feasts are shared with the entire community ('carousing with you'), perhaps during the daytime, which the author apparently finds shocking.

In contrast, in Jude 12, the love feasts are the celebrations of the beloved community, which the ungodly ones blemish or jeopardize when they 'boldly carouse together', perhaps disrupting them with disorderly behavior. Although the language of the two texts is quite similar, the shift in meaning-possibilities is significant. The accepted readings of these texts (*apatais* in 2 Peter, *agapais* in Jude) strongly suggests that 2 Peter is once again clarifying but also significantly modifying Jude. Second Peter's alterations suggest that the community addressed in that letter may not practice a communal meal at all, or they regard those who do celebrate such meals as 'blots and blemishes'.

A less perplexing but also significant shift occurs in relation to the word 'blemishes' in these verses. The word in 2 Pet. 2.13, *spiloi*, may be a correction of Jude 12, where the word *spilades* appears. Perhaps this is comparable to *apatais* as a 'correction' of *agapais*. Kelly argues vigorously that Jude's word *spilas* would be better translated as 'hidden rocks' (1969: 270-271; see also Reese 2000: 112-14) – that is, threats to nautical navigation and therefore belonging to the same category as 'wild waves' and 'wandering stars' (Jude 13). In that case, *spilos* in 2 Pet. 2.13 would contribute to 2 Peter's overall expansion and explanation of Jude, as well as again changing its meaning, and the RSV translators of Jude (along with others, such as KJV) may even be following 2 Peter's lead at this point. See also 2 Pet. 3.14 and Jude 24 (in some manuscript variants), where the words, 'without blemish/ spot [*aspilous, aspiloi*]', appear.

Second Peter's inventory of the uncontrolled, animal-like flaws of the opponents concludes in 2.14-16. Perhaps a hint of 'some who doubt' or who might be saved 'out of the fire' in Jude 22-23 appears in the 'unsteady souls' of 2 Pet. 2.14 (see also 3.16). In an ideological conflict, such people would be the most vulnerable to predators and the least reliable allies, but they would also provide the most obvious battlegrounds between two opposed belief systems or moralities. The people who have 'barely escaped from those who live in error' in 2.18 may be the 'unsteady souls' of 2.14, for if they are recent Christian converts from paganism (see below), they might be more susceptible to the opponents' 'boasts of folly' (see Kelly 1969: 345-348).

Second Peter 2.15-16 considerably expands the cryptic reference in Jude 11 to 'Balaam's error', and the passage also develops the mention of greed in 2.14. The story in Numbers 22–24 does not support this understanding of Balaam, but Num. 31.16 might. In Jewish tradition, as in 2 Pet. 2.15 and perhaps Jude 11, Balaam was often associated with greed (see Kelly 1969: 343). It appears that even the irrational animal that is Balaam's beast of burden can offer a voice of restraint, which makes Balaam and the opponents who 'follow his way' even less than 'a dumb ass'.

The trees, waves, and stars metaphors (with apocryphal overtones) of Jude 12-13 have disappeared from 2 Pet. 2.17, which keeps only the 'nether gloom of darkness'. The 'waterless springs and mists driven by a storm' in this verse may clarify and remove the seeming self-contradiction of 'waterless clouds, carried along by winds' in Jude 12, although clouds of smoke or dust might also be plausible understandings of that phrase. Kelly notes that 2 Peter's image of wind-blown mists 'underline[s] the insubstantiality and flimsiness of the [opponents'] teaching' (1969: 345), and Callan argues that the image 'suggests that the false teachers are controlled by a powerful external force that directs their action' (2003: 59). The thought is continued more directly in 2 Peter 2.18, where 'those who live in error [*planē*]' may echo the 'wandering [*planētēs*]' of the stars in Jude 13 (see also v. 11), even though these stars do not appear in 2 Peter.

Second Peter forcefully concludes its second chapter and its discussion of the opponents with 2.19-22, in which the themes of slavery and freedom are pursued once again. The pronouns are vague in 2.19, for 'They promise *them* freedom, but *they themselves* are slaves' (emphasis added, compare KJV, NRSV, NEB), and the Greek text does not clarify this ambiguity (compare Barthes 1988: 251-255). I understand this sentence to say that the opponents promise freedom but are instead themselves 'slaves [*douloi*] of corruption' (2.19). This may hark back to the opening of 2 Peter, which authoritatively assures the reader that the 'divine power [of Jesus our Lord] has granted to us all things that pertain to life and godliness ... that through these you may escape from the corruption that is in the world because of passion' (1.3-4; see also 1.9).

Perhaps the opponents, like the ones 'who have barely escaped' in 2.18 and on whom they prey, had also once escaped from corruption 'through the knowledge of ... Christ', but they have themselves become again ensnared in 'the defilements of the world' (2.20), 'like irrational animals, creatures of instinct, born to be caught and killed' (2.12). This reading coheres nicely with the proverb in 2.22, which appears to be a double allegory describing the opponents: the 'dog' has purged itself of corruption ('vomit') but then re-defiles itself, and the 'sow' has been baptized ('washed') but then sins again (compare Callan 2009: 112). For these ungodly ones, things are even worse than if they had never known 'the way of righteousness', for now they have knowingly rejected the 'holy commandment' (2.21), whereas before, even in their wrong, pre-Christian ways, they did not know any better. They have no hope, for they cannot repent again and be baptized a second time (see also Jude 12, 2 Pet. 1.9).

These opponents do not sound like gnostics, but they do sound very much like apostates. Despite this, and although both Leaney and Kelly note as much, neither of them sees a conflict with the understanding of the opponents in 2 Peter as gnostics (see Leaney 1967: 126, Kelly 1969: 347-49). While it is conceivable that the opponents might have been non-gnostic Christian converts from paganism ('error', *planē*) who then 'lapsed' from (proto-)orthodoxy into antinomian gnosticism, a less elaborate explanation is also possible: that is, these people have simply returned to their former paganism, which might well also seem 'licentious' to Christians. Indeed, if we do not presuppose, as many readers of 2 Peter do, that the opponents mentioned in that letter are gnostics, then the possibility that they have simply lapsed back into their previous paganism becomes the more plausible option. The hypothesis of gnosticism is unnecessary.

In either case, it is conceivable that the 'freedom' promised by the opponents according to 2 Pet. 2.19 is precisely the same freedom from any master that the ungodly ones in Jude 4 are claiming when they deny the 'Master and Lord'. If 2 Peter's language about slavery to corruption is simply his own hyperbolic 'warning against lapsing' to the reader (Kelly 1969: 347), then the difference between the two letters may not be great, and Jude then even helps us to read 2 Peter (instead of the reverse).

However, once again, the question is not what the people involved really believed, but how these letters depict those beliefs. For 2 Peter, this freedom is illusory, but for Jude it is apparently real. With the exception of 'delivered to them' (2 Pet. 2.21, compare Jude 3), nothing like 2 Pet. 2.19-22 appears in Jude, which does not describe its opponents as slaves of anything, but rather as 'grumblers, malcontents, following their own passions, loud-mouthed boasters, flattering people to gain advantage' (v. 16) – in other words, people who do not respect the 'common salvation' of the community but instead deny 'our only Master and Lord' (vv. 3-4). As I suggested in Chapter 2, they acknowledge no slave-owner at all. These people may or may not be apostate Christians, or antinomians, but they are unlike the opponents in 2 Pet. 2.19, for evidently no master has 'overcome' Jude's ungodly ones, and so they 'look ... after themselves' (Jude 12). In other words, the letter of Jude describes its opponents quite differently than 2 Peter does in this matter of slavery, and even if 2 Peter is a rewriting of Jude, we have no reason to think that they are the same people, or think and act in the same way.

Second Peter's Third Chapter

Second Peter's supposed reworkings of Jude in its first two chapters produce a refinement and clarification of mechanisms of fear and desire embodied in the crucial language of Christ as Master. This is developed further, and taken in a new direction, in 2 Peter's third chapter. At the end of the second chapter there is a break in the flow of argument, and the final chapter opens with a return to themes from the first chapter of the letter: the desire to give the reader a reminder and an 'aroused ... sincere mind' (3.1; see 1.13), with reference to (unnamed) prophets and apostles. In addition, the author claims to have written a previous letter, presumably the one now known as 1 Peter, which may in effect repeat his claim that he is Peter the apostle of Christ (1.1). The confusing language of Jude 17 regarding predictions of the apostles is repositioned in 2 Pet. 3.2 to give it greater sense. Kelly sees 'evidence of the emergence of a NT canon' (or we may go further and say: of the entire Christian Bible) in the conjunction of 'holy prophets' with 'your apostles' who convey 'the commandment of the Lord and Savior' (1969: 354), and I will pursue this question further in the next chapter.

In 2 Pet. 3.3-6, Jude 17-18 is further rewritten in what at the same time serves as a transition to a topic that had only been hinted at earlier, in 1.16. The 'scoffers' (*empaiktēs*) who are 'following their own [Jude: ungodly] passions' are mentioned within the quoted prediction in Jude 18 but appear instead in the main text of 2 Pet. 3.3. Perhaps Jude's scoffers are the grumblers and malcontents of v. 16. In 2 Peter, the scoffers' phrase, 'the fathers fell asleep' (3.4) suggests that, even though the phrase is situated in what appears to be a prophecy of the future, the time period in which the letter was written is indeed well after the first generations of Christians have died.

Perhaps 2 Peter's scoffers are people who have previously charged 2 Peter's author with 'follow[ing] cleverly devised myths' (1.16), prompting his retort (see Kelly 1969: 316, 355). Despite awkward Greek, 2 Peter eliminates the repetition of 'following their own passions' in Jude 16 and 18, and it uses the new quote in 3.4 as an occasion for more comments on the scriptures. These comments apparently refer to Genesis 1 and 6-8 (2 Pet. 3.5-6), but they may also address widespread ancient beliefs about the creative significance of water. The destructive water in 3.6, along with the fire in 3.7, have already been anticipated in 2 Peter's references to the flood and Sodom in 2.5-6.

The end of 2 Peter is also a discussion of the end of days. Second Peter 3.5-9 responds to the scoffers' charge by turning the delay in the coming of the end into evidence for divine patience and mercy. Both the interpretations in 3.5-6 and the quoted scoffing lead to the topic of the return of Christ and the final destruction of the world, themes that do not appear explicitly, and perhaps not even implicitly, in Jude, but which are developed quite graphically in 2 Pet. 3.7-13, although they are anticipated already in 1.11. These verses do not present an interpretation of the scriptures, as earlier in the letter of 2 Peter, or even a reasoned argument of any sort. Instead, they weave together suggestive and not always consistent allusions in order to urge the reader to be patient, and to assure her that the Lord will keep his promise (3.10, 13; see also 1.4) and that the eschatological cataclysm will indeed occur in good time.

'[K]ept until the day of judgment' in 2 Pet. 3.7 echoes Jude 6. However, there is no mention of the Lord's forbearance or the people's repentance in Jude, as there is in 2 Pet. 3.9. The phrase 'like a thief' in 3.10 echoes 1 Thess. 5.2 (but see also Matt. 24.43; Lk. 12.39), where those words are applied to 'the day of the Lord', and where they follow another passage that reassures Christians who may be concerned about the delay of the eschaton (1 Thess. 4.13-18). Second Peter 3.11-12 then challenges the reader to live up to the demands of the coming 'day of God' and rewrites what has just been said at 3.10. This contrasts to Jude 20-21, which also challenges the reader in an exercise of pastoral power ('reinscribing the model's authority while placing the imitator in the position of perpetual unease', Castelli 1991: 110), but which displays no evident apocalyptic overtones. At this point in Jude, the emphasis is on the addressees' faithfulness and patience ('wait ... unto eternal life'), while 2 Peter emphasizes more forcefully their moral character, as though the quality of their lives might even accelerate the eschatological process ('hastening the coming').

This cataclysm, according to 2 Peter, will lead to a new world of righteousness, to which only the 'spotless' ones will presumably be admitted

(3.13-14; see also 1.11). Both Jude 21 and 24 ('present you without blemish before the presence of his glory') also suggest some sort of paradisal life beyond this one, but Jude gives the reader no indication of a coming cataclysm, either imminent or delayed. The phrase, 'new heavens and a new earth' in 2 Pet. 3.13 appears in Isaiah 65-66, and the references to fiery destruction in 2 Pet. 3.7, 10, and 12 may also hint at Jewish scriptures (Zeph. 1.18; 3.8; Mal. 4.1), or they may suggest instead the influence of Hellenistic Stoic thought (see Leaney 1967: 131, Kelly 1969: 361). Kelly claims that 'the idea that the world will be finally annihilated by fire appears only in 2 Peter in the NT, and is indeed in its fully developed form not Biblical at all' (1969: 360).

Neyrey argues that 2 Peter's language suggests that the opponents reject divine providence, and with that a final judgment, the second coming, and life after death, not unlike both Hellenistic Epicurean philosophers and Jewish Sadducees (1980: 414-20). As a result, the opponents claim radical personal freedom ('license'), not unlike the opponents in Jude, and 2 Peter treats this freedom as immorality. It is easy to imagine how either Epicureans or Sadducees might appear as 'licentious', especially in the ad hominem sense noted above, to Christians for whom divine judgment in conjunction with an afterlife was of great importance, as it is in each of these letters (see 2 Pet. 3.7, 13, 17, as well as Jude 3, 21, 24). Rejection of divine providence would especially offend not only 2 Peter's addressees but also others, including pagan Greeks such as the Platonist philosopher Plutarch, as well as the Jewish Pharisees (Neyrey 1980: 418, 423; see Kelly 1969: 301). Kelly suggests that something like this rejection of divine providence on the part of Jude's opponents may also be hinted in v. 16 (1969: 278), but this reading requires a great deal of inference from the text. In any case, the community addressed by the letter of Jude evidently does believe in divine judgment and punishment for the ungodly ones (vv. 4-7, 10-11, 13, 15, 23) as well as mercy for the righteous (vv. 2, 4, 21, 24).

However, none of the material in 2 Pet. 3.8-13 corresponds to anything in the letter of Jude, so that when the phrase from Jude 24, 'without blemish', reappears in an eschatological context in 2 Pet. 3.14 – presumably that of the 'new heavens and a new earth' for which 'we wait' in 3.13 – the significance of the phrase also shifts considerably. The Greek words have also shifted slightly from *amōmous* in Jude to *aspiloi kai amōmētoi* in 2 Peter. In Jude the phrase connotes judgment and the purity of the sacrificial offering, but in 2 Peter it suggests acceptability to enter the new world (see also 1.11). Therefore there are soteriological implications in either case, but not necessarily apocalyptic ones in Jude (Martin 1994: 81, and against Kelly 1969: 291). The word, 'peace', in Jude 2 also reappears in 2 Pet. 3.14, with a similar shift in context and thus meaning.

Although 2 Peter's apocalypticism is often read into Jude, actual evidence for it in that text is hard to find. Kelly understands Jude's metaphor for the ungodly ones, 'twice dead, uprooted' (v. 12), to have apocalyptic connotations (1969: 273), but even that phrase, as Kelly admits, may refer to Christians who have turned away from the correct faith after baptism (apostates). Kelly regards this latter interpretation as acceptable but 'recondite', because he thinks Jude was probably written in the first century (1969: 234). However, there is no reason to think that there were no apostate Christians even in the earliest days of the movement, and there is good reason to think that Jude was written somewhat later. In addition, the phrase, 'the last time', in the quoted words in Jude 18 does not clearly refer to a final destruction of the world (see Kelly 1969: 282-83, as well as 246, and against Martin 1994: 72), or even necessarily to any beliefs of the addressees.

Jude's and 2 Peter's communities may understand phrases such as 'the last time' or 'the last days' in very different ways. (Again, compare Borges's discussion of the relation of Menard's *Quixote* to the text of Cervantes.) There can be little doubt that the community of 2 Peter expects Jesus Christ to return, along with the destruction of this world, even though exactly when that will happen appears to be at least one of the matters that divides the community, and which has been exploited by the opponents (3.4-9, see Desjardins 1987: 98, Callan 2006: 147). Although there is no evidence that the community addressed in Jude does not have similar beliefs, there is also no evidence that they do. There is no mention in Jude's letter of any expectation that Christ will return, or that the world will end in a great cataclysm, or whether any such events will occur sooner or later. Nothing like 2 Peter's descriptions of the final conflagration appears in the letter of Jude, nor does the word *parousia* ('presence' or 'arrival'), which is often used in the New Testament to refer to the return of the son of man or Jesus Christ or the Lord at the end of the world. However, the word *parousia* does occur three times in 2 Peter: in the 'coming of our Lord' (1.16), in the scoffers' denial 'of his coming' (3.4; contrast Jude 18), and in the 'coming of the day of God' (3.12).

Some readers, such as Robert L. Webb, have tried to find allusion to the concept of *parousia* in Jude's citation of 1 *Enoch* in vv. 14-15 (1996: 141-42), but others, such as Ralph P. Martin, suggest that Jude cites 1 *Enoch* as the scriptures of the opponents, not as those of the beloved community (1994: 84, 86). If the latter is the case, then Jude's use of 1 *Enoch* cannot be included as evidence of an apocalyptic inclination. Is it Jude's author who favors Enochian apocalypse, or the opponents? Regardless of the answer, the quote from 1 *Enoch* concerns divine judgment of the ungodly, and while 'the Lord' in that quote (apparently added to the text of 1 *Enoch*) most likely refers to Christ, he 'has come', according to Kelly's translation of *ēlthen* (1969: 276; see also Callan 2003: 59). In other words, the phrase 'the Lord came' in Jude 14 is probably not an announcement of an expected future event, as least in its context in the letter of Jude, but instead it is a description of something that has already happened – or in still other words, it cannot connote the *parousia*. What these words might signify in their larger *1 Enoch* context may be quite different, but that is irrelevant here, for even though the author of Jude explicitly references *1 Enoch* in vv. 14-15, it does not follow from the specifics of that citation alone that anything else is implied about the meaning of the book of *1 Enoch* as a whole.

In addition, Jude's author appears to have removed reference to 'destruction of the ungodly' from his citation of *1 En.* 1.9, focusing on their judgment. Whether this coming of the Lord will coincide with the 'new heavens and a new earth' promised in 2 Pet. 3.13 is not stated in Jude, and to stretch its citation of *1 Enoch* into such an apocalyptic expectation is to read not *1 Enoch* but 2 Peter back into Jude. Indeed, the Enoch citation in Jude contrasts significantly with the 'judgment *and destruction* of ungodly men' in 2 Pet. 3.7 (emphasis added), where there is no evident reference to *1 Enoch*. If 2 Peter did not exist, or at least were not included in the New Testament canon, would readers be so eager to see Jude's references to *1 Enoch*, or other remarks about divine judgment, as apocalyptic? Jude does refer to the punishment of wrongdoers ('the nether gloom', vv. 6, 13; 'fire', vv. 7, 23; see also v. 10), but there is no reason to think that these references are to judgment at the end of the world.

This section of 2 Peter concludes with a reference to 'the forbearance of our Lord as salvation' (3.15), which echoes 3.9 and also serves as a transition to a brief discussion of the letters of 'our beloved brother Paul'. This latter may also be an attempt to confirm the authenticity of 2 Peter. In contrast, there is no reference in the letter of Jude to Paul, and no reason to think that the author of that letter or its addressed community had any knowledge of Paul's letters (or the contrary). Paul mentions Peter in Gal. 2.7-8, but the New Testament evidence regarding a relationship between Peter and Paul is rather limited. As Kelly says, 'Evidently he [the author of 2 Peter] is living at a time when the Apostle's [Paul's] letters, originally dispatched separately to distinct churches or individuals, have begun to be collected together' (1969: 370-71). The indication in 2 Peter that some of Paul's letters have achieved something like scriptural status (3.16) suggests the beginnings of something like a Christian canon (see Chapter 4), and thus serves as evidence that 2 Peter was written well into the second century.

If 'forbearance ... as salvation' refers to a letter attributed to Paul, then it may be Romans (2.4; 9.22) or perhaps 1 Tim. (1.16). That Christians should live morally good lives in expectation of the imminent end of the world is an important theme in several Pauline letters. In addition, there are many Pauline texts, including parts of the letter to the Romans, that might be candidates for the 'things' that are 'hard to understand' in 2 Pet. 3.16. It is well known that Paul's letters were interpreted in many different ways, and Paul himself complains about this (for example, Rom. 3.8). Kelly suggests that 2 Peter is here again attacking the opponents (1969: 373), implying that they 'twist [Paul's letters] to their own destruction', much as they also falsely interpret the other scriptures (see also 1.20-2.1).

In its last two verses, 2 Peter returns once again to topics developed in the first two chapters: the knowledge that the addressed community already has or can develop, and the threats to that knowledge posed by falsehood and passion. The need to guard against error (*planē*, see 2.18) is stressed again in 3.17, and the value of grace and knowledge in 3.18 echoes 1.2. The phrase, 'knowing this beforehand', in 3.17 also echoes Jude 5, 'you were once for all fully informed'. Although concluding doxologies are common in New Testament letters, Jude's final doxology (vv. 24-25) is both more elaborate than 2 Peter's and more typical of the usual practice. As I noted above, 'without blemish' in Jude 24 is transposed to a somewhat earlier position in 2 Peter (3.14), where by way of 'therefore ... since you wait for these' it connects to the apocalyptic content of 3.12-13.

Even though the 'only God' of Jude 25 echoes the 'only Master' of v. 4, as Kelly notes (1969: 292), Jude 25 is clear that God is 'our Savior *through* Jesus Christ [*sōtēri hēmōn dia Iesou Christou*]' (emphasis added) and thereby maintains the distinction between God and Christ. These two instances of 'only' may even serve to emphasize this distinction in Jude: the only God saves through the only Master. This distinction may also lurk behind the doxology of 2 Pet. 3.18, which appears to be addressed to Christ and not to God. Leaney claims that 'This makes the final phrase the only doxology ... in the whole New Testament which is certainly to Christ and not to God' (1967: 139; see also 88), although 2 Tim. 4.18 may be another (debatable) instance. In any case, and as a result, 2 Peter's rewriting of Jude's conclusion again emphasizes their shared distinction between God as opposed to Christ, the only Lord and Master.

What Has 2 Peter Done to Jude?

It is not forbidden to read 2 Peter into Jude, as so many do, and it may not even be unwise, for any number of reasons. Indeed, it may be finally unavoidable. It is now nearly impossible to read these two letters as though they had nothing to do with each other, and perhaps only a genuine Martian could read them in that way. One can only imagine what it would have been like for someone, in the centuries before there was a canon, to read one of these letters without knowing the other. Near the end of his story about Pierre Menard, Borges's nameless narrator says,

> I have thought that it is legitimate to consider the 'final' *Don Quixote* as a kind of palimpsest, in which should appear traces – tenuous but not undecipherable – of the 'previous' handwriting of our friend. Unfortunately only a second Pierre Menard, inverting the work of the former, could exhume and resuscitate these Troys (1962: 54).

To 'unread' or as Borges says 'exhume' 2 Peter from Jude, or vice versa, might require an act of inversion that exceeds any Earthling reader's capabilities, for it would require yet another letter like 2 Peter.

I do not suggest that 2 Peter rewrote Jude in the way that Pierre Menard 'wrote' *Don Quixote*, for although many words appear in both texts, few larger phrases are exactly the same. Nor is this rewriting in the much 'freer' manner in which Joyce rewrote the *Odyssey*. It may have more in common with Kafka's rewritings, although 2 Peter does not display as much writing talent or anything like Kafka's sense of the absurd (see Deleuze and Guattari 1986: 41, 80). In Chapter 2, I noted that it would be tempting to think of the letter of 2 Peter as a 'remake' of Jude, analogous to the 1978 cinematic remake of the 1956 movie, *Invasion of the Body Snatchers*. Movie remakes, like the rewritings of written predecessors, often address 'defects' or unanswered questions that trouble the cinematic 'source text', and thereby they clarify but also change the story, expanding and interpreting it. For example, the 1978 *Body Snatchers* develops and resolves the question, which is left open in the 1956 original, of precisely how the alien seed pods 'snatch' and replace the original person, and it does this in horrifyingly graphic detail. By 'answering' the viewer's questions, the movie may increase the shock value, but it reduces the creepiness and general level of paranoia because it leaves less to the imagination.

As a result of this tendency to explain, it is not unusual for movie remakes to require longer running times than the original, sometimes much longer, and these *Body Snatcher* movies are no exception. The 1956 film is only 80 minutes long, even including the added scenes at its beginning and end, while the 1978 film is 115 minutes long. In this too these films are similar to many rewritten texts: for example, the edition that I have of Joyce's *Ulysses* (1986) is 642 pages long, but my edition of Richmond Lattimore's translation of *The Odyssey* (1967) is only 333 pages, and a Greek edition would very likely be still shorter (since translating is another kind of rewriting). Similarly, the letter of 2 Peter is over twice as long as long as Jude.

Just as 2 Peter 'regularizes' Jude's presentation of the Jewish scriptures (as numerous commentators note), so 2 Peter tends consistently to subdue and tame Jude's extravagant language and frantic tone. As a result, the nervous, unfocused energy of the letter of Jude is replaced by 2 Peter's more finely tuned fears. Jude's slave is anxious to please an all-seeing Master, and apparently she has been confronted by some ancient Karl Marx who tells her that 'you have nothing to lose but your chains'. Second Peter's slave waits eagerly for the vividly depicted but thereby less frightening fiery cataclysm that will accompany the Master's return, along with the day of final reward for those who have remained obedient and punishment of those who have defected to another master.

The prominence of apocalyptic language in the letter of 2 Peter contrasts strongly to its absence from Jude (or near absence, depending on how one reads language such as 'twice dead, uprooted' in v. 12). However, it may also anticipate the persistence of commentators who insist that Jude is apocalyptic anyway. It is as though these readers feel compelled to understand 2 Peter as trying to tell them what Jude 'really means'.

However, this disparity between the letters is not something to be explained away, but instead it describes an important difference between their contents. The letter of 2 Peter is struggling to keep a community 'in line' in the face of a seemingly delayed but inevitable End, while Jude is not seriously concerned about that. Instead, the fear in the letter of Jude is that members of a community are being contaminated (or 'snatched') by ungodly ones. If there is an 'apocalypse' for Jude, it is not the revelation of an end of the world or the *parousia* of Christ, but rather the manifestation of a deadly contagion that threatens to sweep through (and sweep away) the community. Faced with an insidious epidemic of ungodliness, as Jude seems to be, the need to purge all community sites of possible contagion is more important and urgent than preparing for some final cosmic cataclysm.

One consequence of this is that although both of the letters of 2 Peter and Jude themselves vigorously interpret the Jewish scriptures, Jude shows no interest in encouraging either knowledge or interpretation on the part of the community's members. In contrast, 2 Peter's strong emphases on the importance of knowledge and proper (as opposed to 'false') interpretation of the Jewish scriptures and the letters of Paul are not surprising. Scripture and its interpretation plays an important part in both Jewish and Christian apocalyptic thought, and apocalyptic themes are also prominent in Paul's letters. Whether other texts that will eventually appear in the New Testament are also in view, such as the gospels of Matthew or John, is possible but not certain.

To these differences may also be correlated the letter of 2 Peter's admittedly slight tendency to emphasize the importance of proper doctrine more than Jude does. To be sure, in the face of the approaching end of the world it is very important to do the right things, but getting your soul or mind in proper order may be an even higher priority, rather like being prepared for an emergency. Perhaps this is also why 2 Peter approves of self-control, but self-control is a central theme of much Greek philosophy, and the Hellenistic metaphysical or mystical overtones of 2 Peter's language suggests that that too may also be a factor in the letter. In contrast, Jude says nothing positive about self-control, but rather disparages the ungodly ones because they 'look after themselves' (v. 12).

4

The Christian Body and the Christian Mind

To fabricate letters, this is not a question of sincerity but one of functioning. ... That which is the greatest horror for the subject of enunciation [the letter's implied author] will be presented as an external obstacle that the subject of the statement, relegated to the letter, will try at all costs to conquer, even if it means perishing (Deleuze and Guattari 1986: 29, 31).

Desire and its object are one and the same thing: the machine, as a machine of a machine. Desire is a machine, and the object of desire is another machine connected to it (Deleuze and Guattari 1983: 26).

Organ-izing the Christian Body

Along with recognition of Christ as Master, which is a distinctive theme of both the letters of Jude and 2 Peter, comes emphasis on control over the Christian body (see Gorsline 2006: 735), a theme which occupies many of the New Testament letters. This body is both the body of the individual believer, insofar as she submits to the letters' pastoral power and accepts her status as a faithful slave of Christ, and the community as a collective body, what Paul calls 'the body of Christ' (for example, 1 Cor. 12.27), which for each of these letters is seeking to purge itself of some internal contamination.

As early as Jude 4 and 2 Pet. 1.4, the dangers of licentiousness and passion within the Christian community are stressed. The concerns of 2 Peter's author regarding the value of self-control (*egkrateia*, 1.6) reappear later on, in an apocalyptic mode, in themes of godliness, peace, and stability (3.11, 14, 17). Even 2 Peter's allusion to Christ's transfiguration or resurrection or perhaps second coming (1.16-18) connects to this topic of control over the body – in this case, the miraculous body. Also relevant may be 2 Peter's mention of the impending moment when the author will 'put off' his own body, which the letter connects closely to his own desire that the community be able to remember 'these things' (1.13-15). Memory is a function of control, and of the control of bodies, and both Jude and 2 Peter make it clear that the addressed communities already know all that they need to know. Memory plays a crucial role in 'pastoral power', as it does in Nietzschean 'slave morality' (1967: 57-58, see Chapter 1).

The word *egkrateia* does not appear again after 2 Pet. 1.6, and it is rare in the New Testament, appearing elsewhere only in Acts 24.25 and Gal. 5.23. Nevertheless, in the second chapter of 2 Peter, this value becomes a central concern, especially the lack of it in the unrighteous (2.2-3, 7, 10-14, 18-20, 22). Not only is the need for self-control implicit as an ideal in several of 2 Peter's scriptural examples, especially those of Noah and Lot (but also in the 'restraint' provided by Balaam's ass), but as usual the letter's presentation of these matters is itself more controlled than is that of Jude. This should not be surprising, for as I noted in Chapter 3, self-control does not appear to be favored by the letter of Jude. Jude 12 complains that the ungodly ones 'look after themselves', a phrase which more directly asserts that they master (or 'shepherd') themselves, and this fits well with Jude's claim that they reject Christ as their only Master. Furthermore, self-control is absent, not only from Jude's rhetorical extravagances in describing the ungodly ones, but in the paranoia that rages throughout that letter (see Chapter 2).

This matter appears again from another angle. Second Peter's suggestion that believers can work toward salvation in 3.14, 17-18, stands in some tension with the hint of predestination, at least for the opponents, in Jude 4. When Jude 20-21 says, 'beloved, build yourselves up on your most holy faith; pray in the Holy Spirit; keep yourselves in the love of God; wait for the mercy of our Lord Jesus Christ unto eternal life', it seems a rather different thing than when 2 Peter says, 'beloved, since you wait for these, be zealous to be found by him without spot or blemish' (3.14). 'Wait' appears in each statement, but there is less sense in Jude that the believer has any control over events. Jude's statement urges passive waiting (in effect: 'hold on!'), while 2 Peter calls for a more active engagement in securing salvation ('fight the good fight!').

Indeed, the word translated in the Revised Standard Version of Jude 21 as 'wait' is *prosdechomenoi*, 'receive, accept' (Liddell and Scott 1996). Perhaps this element of passivity is a factor that leads some scholars to describe Jude as apocalyptic, but if so, that letter delivers a different sort of revelation from that of 2 Peter. Waiting for an assured end of the world, whether close or distant, is far different from waiting with no expectation of an end, especially if the faithful ones can do something to make the end come sooner, as 2 Pet. 3.12 strongly hints: 'waiting for *and hastening* the coming of the day of God' (emphasis added). That the designation of Jesus Christ as 'Master' has a metaphorical function in 2 Peter, but not in Jude, is also relevant to this different sense of waiting (see Chapter 3).

This overall shift in emphasis is made explicit in 2 Pet. 3.14, where the Greek word translated as 'wait' is *prosdokōntes*, 'expect' (Liddell and Scott 1996). This word appears also in the preceding verse ('according to his promise we wait for new heavens and a new earth'), and in 3.12. The reader is assured that if she presses on faithfully as the Master's slave, then these things will happen for her. It is a guarantee 'according to his promise' (3.13). Although the word in Jude 21, *prosdechomenoi*, can also mean 'expect', the larger message of Jude's letter supports an understanding that the only thing to be done is to remain the faithful slave, and to leave everything in the hands of the Master. Self-control is therefore not a virtue, for Someone Else is controlling you. The chaotic self-shepherding (*poimainontes*, Jude 12) of the opponents results from rejection of the 'good shepherd [*poimēn*]' (Jn 10.11-16), who is the only Master.

In other words, both of these letters seek to control the Christian body, but in significantly different ways. In each case, Michel Foucault's concept of 'pastoral power' is strongly evident, but it functions to a different end and draws upon a different mechanism. According to Gilles Deleuze and Félix Guattari, any given community is dominated by a 'signifying regime' (or what Foucault called the *episteme*, Deleuze and Guattari 1987: 140). Signifying regimes appear in specific forms of discourse and action, which they call 'desiring-machines', mechanisms that both stimulate and control that community's desires. The particular forms vary from one signifying regime to another, but the play of oppositions that they embody remains constant. Even though the communities addressed by these letters appear to be different from one another, a single, more or less homogeneous signifying regime appears in both Jude and 2 Peter, and to this regime correspond desiring-machines that figure both directly and indirectly in each of the letters.

One important machine produces the symbol of the Lord Jesus Christ as Master. A second machine is very closely coupled to it, and this machine produces the symbol of the faithful or 'godly' believer as Slave. These two machines function together in each letter as a single composite unit, an assemblage, each member of which depends on the operation of the other. As a result of the operations of this regime, the opponents in both Jude and 2 Peter appear as saboteurs who threaten the function of the master-slave assemblage by offering 'lines of flight' or escape from the organized Christian body. However, the precise nature of this threat is one point at which the letters diverge, as two different lines of flight are described in them. While 2 Peter's ungodly ones seek to lure the believers to a different master-slave system (perhaps paganism, perhaps Christian heresy), the opponents in Jude apparently reject every master-slave mechanism and call for freedom from any master whatsoever.

Still other desiring-machines connect to the master-slave machinery in each of the letters, again with differing results. One considerable distinction between the letters concerns desire for an end to the world and for 'new heavens and a new earth', 'the day of God' (2 Pet. 3.12-13) accompanied by Christ's eternal kingdom. As I have noted already, this machine plays a significant role in 2 Peter but little if at all in Jude, and this difference also has consequences for the master-slave assemblage in each case.

Through these desiring-machines, the uncoded material stuff of the 'body without organs' is structured or 'reterritorialized' in the letters of Jude and 2 Peter into Christianity. Deleuze and Guattari's phrase, 'body without organs' (borrowed from Antonin Artaud [1976: 571]), refers to the 'smooth' flow of matter apart from any communicable characteristics, or in their words, 'the *field of immanence* of desire' (1987: 154, their emphasis). It is the meaningless that-ness of everything that is actual. Except as an unavoidable remainder, the body without organs or schizophrenic body cannot be known as such. 'You never reach the Body without Organs, you can't reach it, you are forever attaining it, it is a limit' (1987: 149-150). Although the body without organs must be presupposed for any thought or utterance whatsoever, it can only be encountered through an already-coded system (that is, something that it is not), a signifying regime through which meaningless bodies are *organ*-ized into meaningful *organ*-isms, such as the self, human society, or the world.

Desiring-machines encode or decode the endless flow of meaningless matter that is the body without organs, transforming it into a meaningful self and world, which is the 'full body' (Deleuze and Guattari 1983: 281). The full body is the world and all its components as both product and object of desire, and therefore desire is always already there, incarnated in the human world. The signifying regime inevitably transforms the body without organs into the full body, encoding and thereby organizing it into religious, aesthetic, or scientific objects that we understand and describe, seek or avoid. As I described in Chapter 2, this organization is always, in the terminology of Deleuze and Guattari, 'paranoid'. This is another, even more abstract but equally potent way to describe pastoral power. Lines of flight will always break free from or in any organized body, but such drives for freedom will always be reclaimed by desire and its machines (Deleuze and Guattari 1986: 35). The full, paranoid body is all that we can know, and therefore our world is always a meaningful world.

The production of reality occurs when language carves the body without organs into a signifying regime of functional units (organs of the full body), and this is precisely what the letters of Jude and, perhaps more successfully, 2 Peter are doing – or rather, it is what they do when read within a canonical or any other meaningful context. Some of Jude's metaphors for the ungodly, especially 'wild waves' and 'wandering stars' (v. 13) suggest the chaos of a 'smooth', disorganized body, although self-control in the form of 'looking after oneself' is a characteristic of the ungodly ones in Jude 12, and this too implies some form of organization, but not that of the 'beloved in God the Father'.

Jude itself, as a letter, is far less organized than 2 Peter is. As I noted in Chapter 2, what unites Jude's metaphors of non-control and its hatred of the self-shepherding of the ungodly ones is their rejection of Christ as Master. However, Jude is not a call *for* (self-)control but rather an attempt *to* control the spreading contamination. In contrast, by omitting Jude's images of disorganized chaos and adding further language that implies an opposition between different full or organized bodies, such as Lot versus Sodom (2.6-7) or slaves of Christ versus slaves of corruption (2.19), 2 Peter depicts a conflict between two alternative systems of organization: either slavery to Christ, or slavery to corruption. These alternatives provide the context for 2 Peter's emphases on self-control and the coming of the eschaton.

Another desiring-machine in 2 Peter invokes apostolic tradition and authority, with special focus on the apostles Peter and (less forcefully) 'our beloved brother Paul' (3.15). Second Peter also calls for carefully controlled interpretation of 'the scriptures [*graphē*]' (1.20; see also 3.16), and this may include some Christian texts as prophecy and perhaps even canon. The saints and apostles function in a somewhat different machine in Jude, for only James (probably not the disciple, and if the allusion is to the brother of Jesus, not exactly an apostle) appears by name (v. 1; see also v. 17). Furthermore, the word 'scripture' does not appear in Jude, although the letter refers numerous times to Jewish scriptures. This scripture-machine includes both *1 Enoch* and the Assumption of Moses (and no evident Christian texts), and it produces different results than the machine that is 2 Peter. In other words, the scriptures organize a somewhat different body in Jude.

Canon Effect

Considered by itself, as it probably once existed and perhaps was circulated (even if not in its present form) for at least some time before the letter of 2 Peter was written, the letter of Jude's semiotic failings and breakdowns are readily apparent. Furthermore, even though 2 Peter goes a long way toward remedying some of Jude's deficiencies, and despite its much greater length, 2 Peter's 'revision is at times more obscure than the Jude material with which he began' (Callan 2003: 63). In part this may be due to the apparent lesser skill as a writer of 2 Peter's author, and in part to the letter's shifting of focus away from that of Jude even as it continues to use much of Jude's material. Each letter presents serious problems of coherence and comprehensibility to the reader – problems of expression – entirely apart from (although often related to) the problems that readers might have with its ethical or theological content. In each case this failure of meaning profoundly threatens the organization of the Christian body.

To some degree any written text will be ambiguous and incomprehensible, and these problems arise from the text's very nature as a writing. Written texts are always more obscure and ambiguous than spoken words. Some portion of the material flow or body without organs is always uncoded and even uncodable, and it escapes the desiring-machines (Deleuze and Guattari 1983: 163, 173). The organization and limitation of the coded flows itself cannot prevent at least some failure of signification, and it may even result in the breakdown of the signifying regime itself. For this reason, people have mistrusted written texts for perhaps as long as the technology of writing has been known. For an explicit example of this mistrust in the Bible, see 2 Cor. 3.1-6.

However, these problems are more apparent in some written texts than they are in others. The body without organs is never completely encoded; in other words, no paranoia can ever be exhaustive or unassailable, and there are always possibilities for schizophrenic chaos. Deleuze and Guattari claim that 'it is the displacement of the limit that haunts all societies, the displaced represented that disfigures what all societies dread absolutely as their most profound negative: namely, the decoded flows of desire' (1983: 177). It is this fear that haunts both Jude and 2 Peter, and this is the same fear that haunts every witch hunt and attack on heresy or difference: the fear that the infection or pollution introduced and augmented by the ungodly ones (or in more modern terms, Communists, Jews, blacks, homosexuals, feminists, etc.) has already spread so far throughout the community that only total destruction can completely eradicate it, as in 2 Pet. 3.10 ('dissolved with fire'). The Christian body can never be fully or finally secured by any text, or by any amount of text.

As I noted in Chapter 1, the Christian canon arises, in part at least, from desire to control the interpretation of the scriptures. The canon is another desiring-machine, and one of its functions is to control the unlimited meaning-possibilities (schizophrenia) of writings that have been given the special, authoritative status of 'scripture' (for every writing is scripture in the broadest sense). On a much larger scale than either Jude or 2 Peter, the New Testament responds to the threat of 'decoded flows of desire', and it attempts to establish a single 'Word of God' (as in 2 Pet. 3.5, 7). This Word will decisively secure the organized Christian body, both the individual believer and the whole body of Christ. In this respect, either Jude or 2 Peter alone (but even more so, both of them together) offers a miniature version of the desire manifested in the Christian canon – that is, the desire to control the interpretation of the scriptures so as to produce an authoritative message.

As I also noted in Chapter 1, each of these letters themselves had some difficulty entering the New Testament canon, and Jude especially so. It seems

likely that if 2 Peter had never been written, Jude's chances of receiving
canonical acceptance would have been very small. Second Peter in effect
transforms Jude, making its paranoia more reasonable, and the result is in
some ways comparable – although both the techniques and the content
involved are quite different – to the gospel of Matthew's transformation of
Mark, or the gospel of Luke's transformation of both of those gospels (see
Callan 2004: 63-64). If the gospel of Luke had not been written, the odds
that Mark would have been included in the canon along with Matthew go
down. Alternatively, if the gospel of Matthew had not been written, the
odds that Mark would have been included in the canon along with Luke
go down. In other words, the fact that both Matthew and Luke were widely
accepted required the idea of multiple gospels, and this increased Mark's
chances of canonical acceptance as well, since Mark shares much with
either or both of them.

However, in the present case, there are only two texts involved. I suspect that if the letter of Jude had never been written, then 2 Peter (had it
somehow been written anyway) would have also had a much harder time
getting into the canon. Let us suppose that Jude had disappeared soon after
2 Peter rewrote it, rather like the supposed 'Q' text that scholars use to
explain material that appears in both Matthew and Luke but not in Mark.
Unlike the letter of Jude, there is no evidence for Q's existence apart from
the strong similarities between Matthew and Luke, against Mark. Although
the letter of 2 Peter is clearly more theologically suitable to the canon, and
Christian belief, than is Jude, nevertheless a second text, also claiming to
have been written by an apostle or at least someone very close to Christ and
also strikingly similar in both expression and content to 2 Peter, would have
counted in favor of including both of them in the New Testament, no matter how unsuitable either of them is by itself. Otherwise, both letters would
have had to be rejected.

In addition, desire for correct interpretation and even something like
desire for a canon are explicit features of 2 Peter, as I noted in Chapters 1
and 3 (see also Martin 1994: 145, 149, 161). The conjunction of the apostles
of early Christianity with the prophets of the Jewish scriptures in 2 Pet. 3.2
echoes Eph. 2.19-20 ('you are fellow citizens with the saints and members of
the household of God, built upon the foundation of the *apostles and prophets*,
Christ Jesus himself being the cornerstone', emphasis added). These texts
anticipate the two divisions of the Christian Bible, with 'the prophets' being
the Old Testament and 'the apostles' being the New Testament. Second
Peter and Ephesians become precursors of the canonical desiring-machine.

Although Jude mentions the saints in v. 3 and the apostles in v. 17, that
letter never mentions the prophets as such (except for the passing and not
at all positive reference to Balaam). However, perhaps even Jude's apparent

violations of the desire for a canon (through its references to the apocryphal *1 Enoch* and the Assumption of Moses) may connect to that desiring-machine. By constructing a somewhat different machine, what Jude includes becomes a foil against which 2 Peter's inclusions are to be preferred. Again, a comparable situation appears in the 'canon' that was advocated by the second century Christian, Marcion. Marcion's list was eventually rejected by other Christians, but his efforts contributed to the emerging desire for a Christian canon. Unlike Jude's apocryphal preferences, Marcion's chosen texts (Luke and the letters of Paul, perhaps in somewhat different form) did make it into the canon, but along with many others, including the entire Old Testament.

Despite or even because of their theological oddities and strange language, the letters of 2 Peter and Jude form a strange, mini-canonical 'couple', perhaps even to be read together, much as the synoptic gospels or the letters of Paul are often read together. The 'sense' that appears between Jude and 2 Peter even grounds a sort of 'canon effect' – that is, the effect on meaning that results from including certain texts in a highly exclusive and authoritative collection. In the present case, what seems to be both a source text and its rewritten 'version' appear within the single unity of the Bible, and the result is a new thing, a kind of fusion of the texts. Similar phenomena appear between several other pairs of texts or even larger groupings of books in the Bible. Among the synoptic gospels, either Luke or Matthew makes sense of Mark (although not always the same sense), and Luke and Matthew make sense of each other. When John is added to the other three gospels, the sense shifts again. The Pauline letters are also often read as though they are little more than chapters (or versions) of a single, more comprehensive letter.

The second-century Christian, Tatian, went so far as to physically rewrite the four gospels into a single text, known as the *Diatesseron* ('through the four'), and this fusion also suggests that people were wanting by that time to read the various books as though they belonged together as parts of a single, larger book. A harmonization such as this is a different sort of meaning-machine than a canon, but the result may sometimes be similar. Like Marcion's very narrow canon, Tatian's harmony of the four gospels was eventually rejected by the Christian churches. However, by the third century, Christians were collecting the gospels, or the Pauline letters, or the catholic letters, bound together in pre-canonical manuscript codexes. Second Peter's reference to 'all his [Paul's] letters' (3.16) may even be early evidence of such a collection (see Kelly 1969: 370-71). Since the codex book format made the concept of canon also desirable as a practical tool – that is, a single volume containing the entire Bible – these early collections may also be symptoms of desire for a canon. In effect, they form proto-canons.

Several such 'couples' (or in some cases, 'multiples'), collections of texts in which both the apparent revision and the 'original' often appear side by side, have been included within the Bible's canonical enclosure. Not only the two letters of 2 Peter and Jude and the three synoptic gospels, Luke, Matthew, and Mark, but also Ephesians and Colossians in the New Testament, Chronicles and Kings in the Old Testament, and even crossing testamental lines, Revelation and Daniel – all of these fit this pattern. We might also add Deuteronomy as a 'couple' with Exodus–Numbers. These phenomena also suggest political compromises between groups with differing interests.

The New Testament itself serves as a canonical 'couple' with the Old Testament. The addition to the emerging Christian canon of an entire second testament – for despite the tendency of some modern Christians to call it the 'First Testament', the Old Testament has always been the secondary one to Christians – also contributes to the canon effect described above. In order to transform the Jewish scriptures into the Old Testament, another kind of rewriting of the texts had to occur, much more radical than that between Jude and 2 Peter, not quite the act of a Pierre Menard (see Chapter 3) and yet perhaps even more absurd and grandiose (see Hebrews 8.6-7; 9.15; 12.24). These books then become Christian writings, not writings by Christians but writings for Christians, in which the Christ or Son of God of the New Testament has been prophetically announced and a meaning-filled context for his life, teachings, and death has been provided.

On one hand, perhaps this multiplying of texts is some kind of canonical self-critique, or even self-parody, a recognition of the multiplicity of truths and a celebration of difference. Some readers have argued as much, especially in relation to the gospels. However, it is only in the last few decades that numerous readers have begun to read these texts in this way, or to value such a reading. On the other hand, this is one of several ways that the canon controls the meanings of its constituent texts, restraining and taming the usually wilder 'originals' by including them in the collection – that is, providing the proper context in which they should be read. It is one way in which the body (only now it is the body of 'the scriptures') is organized. However, further study is needed of the tensions that appear between the texts in each of these clusters, and of how the texts involved function together as clusters within the larger canon-machine. For example, although the relation between the letters of 2 Peter and Jude is not unlike that between the gospels of Luke and Mark, it is also by no means the same.

Theology and the Gospel

The canon of scriptures and its effects on the reading of texts has been a recurrent topic in this book. The reader, perhaps especially if she is an 'outsider' (a Martian, as in the Preface), will be more aware of the impact of the canon on the reading of books that are in some tension with its controls, such as the letters of Jude and 2 Peter, than in the case of texts such as the undisputed Pauline letters or the gospel of Luke, which contribute in important ways to the larger canon effect (see Aichele 2011: 187-214). In addition, the tendency of many modern readers to treat Jude and to some degree also 2 Peter as nothing but attacks on early gnostic antinomianism makes it easy to dismiss these letters as irrelevant to the modern world. Other readers use these letters as grist for their own morality mills, resulting perhaps in a different sort of marginalization. Each of the letters itself encourages either treatment, both positively in vague attacks on 'licentiousness' and 'ungodliness' along with the ubiquitous paranoia, and negatively by its overall lack of detailed descriptions of either the addressed communities or the attacked opponents. As I noted in Chapter 1, both Jude and 2 Peter are in effect 'form letters' for hatred of difference.

Reading a written text always brings to the fore the question of its meaning or message, and if the reader's desire for meaning is not quickly satisfied, that makes her even more aware of that challenge. In relation to scriptural texts, this desire often takes on a theological form. However, as James D.G. Dunn notes, 'the traditional style of studying a New Testament document is by means of straight exegesis, often verse-by-verse. Theological concerns jostle with interesting historical, textual, grammatical and literary issues, often at the cost of the theological' (1994: ix). Dunn's statement is reminiscent of some words of Roland Barthes: 'The theologian would no doubt be distressed by this indecision [between alternative hypotheses regarding the meaning of a text]; the exegete would acknowledge it, hoping that some element, factual or argumentative, would allow him to bring it to an end' (1988: 251). Barthes goes on to say that 'the textual analyst, it must be said, if I may judge by my own impression, will savor this sort of friction between two intelligibilities'. Barthes writes these words following his own textual analysis of the story of Jacob wrestling in Genesis 32, but I think that his words apply equally well to the analysis of either Jude or 2 Peter.

In the letters of Jude and 2 Peter, theologians may be particularly distressed by their messages, while many exegetes find some comfort in withdrawing into historical discussions of them, thereby avoiding the questions of their theologies. Rarely is there any 'savoring of friction'. Dunn's statement comes from his introduction to Andrew Chester's and Ralph P. Martin's book, *The Theology of the Letters of James, Peter, and Jude*. Despite (or perhaps as an illustration of) this statement, even Martin's discussion of the theology of Jude and 2 Peter in that book often only minimally addresses theological concerns, while historical and literary matters occupy center stage. This is not a criticism of Martin's chapters, and his discussion of these letters is not atypical. Indeed, insofar as either of those letters addresses specifically theological matters at all, the result is often not particularly illuminating.

However, each of these letters does have some positive theological content. In each one a God-simulacrum appears, and in each one a Jesus Christ-simulacrum also appears. The Holy Spirit is also described either as that in which people pray (Jude 20; see also 19) or which moves people to 'speak from God' (2 Pet. 1.21), but God and Jesus Christ are more fully described. In each letter, God is 'the Father' (Jude 1; 2 Pet. 1.17), but Christ is not referred to in either of them as 'the Son', except for 2 Pet. 1.17, where the designation appears in a quotation attributed to 'the voice ... borne to him by the Majestic Glory' and may be equivalent to 'honor and glory from God the Father'. Furthermore, the echo between 'my beloved Son' in 1.17 and 2 Peter's several references to the community as 'beloved' (3.1, 8, 14, 17) may imply that they all regard themselves as God's children – that is, that Christ is not unique in this regard. Each of the letters describes Jesus Christ as 'the Lord', and although his status is quite god-like in each of them, it is rather clearly not one of identity to, or unity with God.

Although trinitarian thought may be incipient in either or both of these letters, it is far from fully formed. It is not hard to imagine how this language could be developed into a trinitarian view, but it also does not demand such a view in either case (contrast Matt. 28.19, and see also 2 Cor. 13.14 and 1 Pet. 1.2). Such 'dyadic and triadic patterns ... represent a pre-reflective and pre-theological phase of Christian belief' and appear also in the writings of second century proto-orthodox 'apostolic fathers' such as Clement of Rome, Justin, and Ignatius (Kelly 1960: 90). Therefore this language may provide still more evidence of a relatively late date for these letters.

For Jude and 2 Peter, God is at the center of proper faith ('godliness'), and God both loves and judges all, condemning sinners and rescuing or 'keeping' the righteous. This latter is particularly emphasized in 2 Peter (2.5, 7, 9; see also 3.15). However, although there is no evident inconsistency between the letters' two God-simulacra, it is also not clear that they are the same. Second Peter's God is closely associated with its apocalyptic message, for in that letter God both created and will destroy the world (3.5-6, 12). It is God, not Christ, who performs the mythic tasks in 2 Peter (2.4-7; 3.5-7), and who will do so again on the 'day of God' (2.9; 3.9-12). Nevertheless, despite Jerome Neyrey's claim that theology is more significant in 2 Peter than Christology (1980: 430), even though God is the savior of believers, he saves them through Christ (2 Pet. 1.1; 3.18; see also Jude 1, 21, 25). In contrast, Jude's God plays a much less prominent part in that letter, appearing only in close association with Christ, who is the sole agent of God's grace (vv. 4, 25; see also 2 Pet. 1.2; 3.18).

However, although God is the Father in both letters, he is only nominally in charge for either of them, for only Jesus Christ is strictly speaking the 'Master and Lord' (Jude 4). There are important distinctions to be made between these two Christ-simulacra. The letter of Jude says nothing about Jesus' life, death, or resurrection, but as 'the Lord', Jude's Christ-simulacrum saved a people out of Egypt (v. 5), rebuked the devil in Michael's words (v. 9), and came with holy myriads according to the quote from *1 Enoch* (v. 14). Thereby Christ acquires a mythic and superhuman quality in that letter. In contrast, 2 Peter mentions the transfiguration (unless 1.17-18 alludes to the resurrection or perhaps the *parousia*), and something like the post-resurrection story of the prediction of Peter's death in Jn 21.18-19 (2 Pet. 1.14). For 2 Peter, Jesus Christ is powerful and coming (1.16), and he welcomes believers into his eternal kingdom (1.11, contrast Jude 21, 24-25), to which they achieve entrance through effective knowledge of him (1.3-8; 2.20; 3.17-18). As 'the Lord and Savior', Christ issues commandments through apostles such as Peter himself (1.1; 3.2). Again, these two simulacra are not obviously incompatible, but they are also not obviously the same.

As the Master, Jesus Christ keeps the righteous ones as his slaves, and they owe him unwavering faithfulness, according to both letters. Jude does not say how the believers became Christ's slaves, but 2 Peter indicates that Christ bought them, probably from powers of 'corruption' in the world (2.1, 19-20) which were their prior owners. Once again, the master-slave language in 2 Peter is clearly metaphorical, but this metaphoric quality is not evident in Jude (see Chapters 2 and 3). In 2 Peter the Jesus Christ-simulacrum is strongly connected by way of this metaphor to the question of salvation, but any such connection in Jude is much less certain.

In the Preface to this book, I described the crucial message of salvation that Christianity proclaims to its own believers as well as to the larger world as the Gospel of Jesus Christ, the signified content of the Bible as 'Word of God'. This Gospel appears only vaguely at best in either Jude or 2 Peter, and this may be why J.N.D. Kelly claims, in his huge commentary on the letters of Peter and Jude, that 'the gospel message does not shine very luminously through them' (1969: 225). The Greek word *euaggelion* ('gospel'), which is one of Paul's favorite words, does not appear in either Jude or 2 Peter (contrast 1 Pet. 4.17), and nothing like Paul's 'gospel' is evident in either of the letters, despite 2 Peter's evident approval of 'all his [Paul's] letters' (3.16). For Paul, 'the gospel' refers to divine grace which saves the believer through her faith in the death and resurrection of Jesus Christ (for example, Rom. 1.16). In contrast, the dominant concern throughout the letters of Jude and 2 Peter has more to do with the challenge presented to pastoral power by contaminations of 'ungodliness', and the paranoia that responds to it.

Since Paul's letters play a major part in the larger message of the New Testament canon, and especially the biblical message of the Gospel of Jesus Christ, what results in either Jude or 2 Peter is a 'mixed message'. The phrase 'Jesus Christ' is quite common in both Jude and 2 Peter, as it is in

Paul's letters (although he prefers 'Christ Jesus'), but there is no 'gospel' for either Jude or 2 Peter. Of the two letters' positive content, only the shared description of Jesus Christ as Master – that is, as slave-owner – is a significant addition to the Gospel message of the New Testament, but whether that is a positive addition is certainly debatable, as the ambivalence of Kelly among others indicates.

Despotēs is used in relation to Christ in the New Testament only in the letters of Jude and 2 Peter. As I noted in Chapter 2, the writings of Paul are equivocal at best in their descriptions of Christians as slaves, and Paul never uses *despotēs*. In other words, apart from this 'contribution' (if we may call it that), if neither the letter of Jude nor that of 2 Peter had been included in the New Testament, then the overall canonical message, the Word of God, would not have been affected at all. Indeed, although neither of these letters is overtly inconsistent with or contradictory to the Gospel, they both require substantial supplementation from the rest of the Bible, and from the larger fields of Christian thought and discourse, in order to be united with the larger Word of God and to manifest their relevance to modern Christianity. This supports the thought that the inclusion of these letters in the canon might have been at least as much to control their wild meaning-possibilities as it was due to their claims to possess apostolic credentials.

However, even though Jude and 2 Peter may contribute nothing helpful to the biblical message, the 'canon effect' of these two letters, described above, may do some harm. Canonical control may backfire. One consequence of the inclusion of these letters in the New Testament is that the currents of fear and paranoia that drive both Jude and 2 Peter may themselves contaminate the entire canon-machine, tainting each text that it controls in the Christian reading. In other words, the two authors' own fears of contamination may have themselves infected the Word of God, not with the opponents' heresies, but with their own fears of difference.

Perhaps this is also why these letters have both been so widely ignored, and why those who do read them tend to assume that the authors and addressed communities are the 'good guys', who will eventually be known as orthodox Christians, and that the infiltrators must then be the 'bad guys' (Desjardins 1987: 92). Such exclusions are required by a paranoid despotic regime (see Chapter 2). While we may not be able to blame this much directly on these letters, both Robert Seesengood (2007) and Terrance Callan (2009: 113), commenting on 2 Peter's use of animal metaphors to refer to the opponents (2.12, 22; see also Jude 10), note the potential that such texts offer to support or even encourage practices of human degradation (see also Martin 1994: 163, Gorsline 2007: 735, Countryman 2007: 751). Perhaps some other biblical texts equal or even exceed the narrow exclusiveness and hatred of difference that are strong in Jude and in 2 Peter, but no other biblical text connects this paranoia so directly or explicitly to the thought of a canon.

Reading with Different Assumptions

I have repeatedly noted Michel Desjardins's claim that scholars often assume that the opponents in both Jude and 2 Peter are gnostic heretics, and they then read that assumption into the language of those letters (1987). Since the identity of the addressed community as well as that of the attacked opponents is of great importance in understanding each of these letters, these topics occupy a great deal of the scholarly attention that has been paid to them. As a final thought-experiment, I want to invert the supposition that Desjardins challenges. Let us suppose that the opponents who are attacked in these letters are somewhat different groups of oth-erwise (proto-)orthodox Christians, who because they are different from the addressed communities of Jude and 2 Peter appear to be 'ungodly' and 'heretic' to the letters' authors. In other words, suppose that the writers and first recipients of these letters would themselves most probably be regarded by other Christian readers, perhaps even ourselves, as 'heretics'. How would this affect our understanding of these letters?

Since the different communities addressed by the letters of Jude and 2 Peter both clearly distinguish between God and Jesus Christ, then perhaps the opponents that these letters find dangerous are the sort of Christians who blur that distinction. Such Christians might celebrate the virginal con-ception and divine sonship of Jesus Christ as described in the gospel of Luke. Perhaps they would even be quite content to call Jesus both Lord and Christ but nevertheless refuse to call him 'Master'. (*Despotēs* appears in Lk. 2.29 and Acts 4.24, but each time in reference to God.) These Christians might even deny that they are anyone's slaves, or perhaps they would prefer instead something more like Gal. 3.28, 'there is neither slave nor free, ... for you are all one in Christ Jesus'. Surely Jude's author, and probably 2 Peter's author as well, would not approve of that verse. Again, simply because each group of opponents denies that Christ is the Master, it does not necessarily follow that either of them denies that Jesus is Christ.

Alternatively, perhaps instead of Luke, it is the gospel of John that the opponents read. John's Jesus is the incarnate divine Word, and 'we have beheld his glory' (1.1-5, 14). This Jesus even says, 'I and the Father are one' (10.30), and he abounds in glory. Perhaps this, not nocturnal ejaculation, is the meaning of the claim in Jude 8 that the ungodly or unrighteous ones 'in their dreamings defile the flesh [*sarx*, the same word used in Jn 1.14]' (compare 2 Pet. 2.10) and 'revile the glorious ones'. In other words, the opponents' sin is not that they are unorthodox, but that they are indeed orthodox (or they will be, in due time).

To be sure, this supposition would be inconsistent with Neyrey's comparison of the opponents in 2 Peter to Epicureans or to Sadducees (1980: 414-20). However, even this inconsistency might be avoided if instead of simply rejecting divine providence, the opponents have interpreted the idea of the 'day of judgment' as something other than a future historical cataclysm. Both the gospels of Luke and John tend to downplay the apocalyptic dimensions of their Jesuses' words (in comparison to Matthew or Mark), and each of them anticipates a triumphant, universal Church, not the imminent destruction of the world. Luke's Jesus even says 'many will come in my name, saying, ... 'The time is at hand!' Do not go after them. ... the end will not be at once' (21.8-9), and John's Jesus says, 'My kingship is not of this world' (18.36). In a similar vein, some of the gnostics understood Paul as referring to a 'spiritual' resurrection of the believer, according to Kelly (1969: 374).

On this reading, the problem that 2 Peter addresses would not be that the opponents deny the apocalypse altogether but rather that they do not give it correct emphasis. Luke and John do not deny divine providence, but they offer significantly different understandings of it. Nor do they reject the idea of an end of the world, or even of a delay in the end (as 2 Peter may, see 3.8-9), but they do not use the extravagant language of flood and fire that 2 Peter favors. They do not say what the scoffers say in 2 Pet. 3.4, but again, these are the letter's words, not necessarily an accurate quotation. To 2 Peter's community, the gospels of Luke and John might appear to be 'scoffing'. The 'prophecies of scripture' in those texts would be matters of their own interpretation, as described in 2 Peter 1.19-20, especially if Callan's understanding of the Greek text is correct (2006: 147-49, but see Porter and Pitts 2008). Similar divergent views might also account for 2 Peter's concern regarding the proper interpretation of Paul's letters in 3.15-16.

Finally, perhaps these supposed proto-orthodox opponents regularly celebrate the sacrificial death of Christ at eucharistic meals, during which they ritually eat the body and drink the blood of 'the Lord'. If such a meal were celebrated as part of (or in conjunction with) a 'love feast' of Jude's community, would it appear to the author of Jude as a 'blemish' on that feast, a 'bold carousing, looking after themselves'? Would such a eucharistic meal appear to the author of 2 Peter as a 'daytime revel' or 'dissipation'? Would the charges of 'licentiousness' be any less appropriate, even though they arose from the writers' sense that these other Christians live a very different life – a very different Christianity – perhaps too different to be tolerated?

As it appears that the communities to which these letters were addressed were different from each other, and that the opponents whom they attack were also different, how is it that a common vocabulary and even to some degree a common conceptual framework would suffice for both? Both communities are dominated by versions of the master-slave desiring-machine – they share the same signifying regime – and despite the important differences that have been mentioned in the preceding chapters, 2 Peter's community is sufficiently similar to Jude's community that a 'poaching' of Jude's letter would be feasible. Perhaps it is that, more than anything else, that defines these communities as Christians, but a sort of Christian (especially the ones addressed by the letter of Jude) that many modern Christians, whether Protestant, Catholic, or Orthodox, would regard as considerably different than themselves.

In order to justify this reversed assumption, one would still have to account for the eventual inclusion of the letters of Jude and 2 Peter in the Christian canon. Why would the emerging mainstream of orthodox Christianity adopt these letters that had earlier attacked them? Indeed, this would not be any more difficult than under the dominant assumption. As I noted in Chapter 1, that inclusion was a difficult one, and quite probably only made possible by the apostolic claims made by the letters. We know that at least some early Christian writers did approve of Jude and 2 Peter, prior to the formation of the canon, and as I noted above, 2 Peter even encourages the idea of a Christian canon. Furthermore, there are reasons to believe that other texts that might have been unpalatable theologically (such as the gospel of Mark, or the Old Testament book of Ecclesiastes) were included in the Christian canon in order to restrain or contain their unruly contents by situating them in a suitably Christian context for reading. There can be little doubt that Jude and 2 Peter, each in its own way, allows for a more orthodox reading, especially when read in the canonical context, as the history of Christian commentaries on these letters demonstrates.

This thought-experiment then leaves two possibilities open. Either the letters of Jude and 2 Peter were written to counter gnostic or other Christian heretics, as the vast majority of scholars believe, despite rather skimpy and uncertain evidence (which is summarized in Chapter 1). Or else the opponents were not heretics, and if that were the case, then there is at least some reason to think that they were instead proto-orthodox Christians, and that it was the letter writers and their addressees who were, from the standpoint of emergent Christian orthodoxy, the 'heretics'.

BIBLIOGRAPHY

Aichele, George

2001   *The Control of Biblical Meaning: Canon as Semiotic Mechanism*. Harrisburg, PA: Trinity Press International.

2006   *The Phantom Messiah: Postmodern Fantasy and the Gospel of Mark*. London: T. & T. Clark International.

2011   *Simulating Jesus: Reality Effects in the Gospels*. London: Equinox.

Artaud, Antonin

1976   *Selected Writings*. Trans. and ed. Helen Weaver and Susan Sontag. New York: Farrar, Strauss, Giroux.

Barrow, Geoff, Beth Gibbons, and Adrian Utley (composers)

1994   'Wandering Star', from the Portishead album, *Dummy*. London: Go! Discs.

Barthes, Roland

1967a   *Elements of Semiology*. Trans. Annette Lavers and Colin Smith. New York: Hill & Wang.

1967b   *Writing Degree Zero*. Trans. Annette Lavers and Colin Smith. New York: Hill & Wang.

1974   *S/Z*. Trans. Richard Miller. New York: Hill & Wang.

1977   *Roland Barthes*. Trans. Richard Howard. New York: Hill & Wang.

1979   *The Eiffel Tower and Other Mythologies*. Trans. Richard Howard. New York: Hill & Wang.

1983   *The Fashion System*. Trans. Matthew Ward and Richard Howard. Berkeley and Los Angeles: University of California Press.

1986   *The Rustle of Language*. Trans. Richard Howard. Berkeley and Los Angeles: University of California Press.

1988   *The Semiotic Challenge*. Trans. Richard Howard. New York: Hill & Wang.

Bauckham, Richard

1983   *Jude, 2 Peter*. Word Biblical Commentary, 50. Waco, TX: Word Books.

Bauer, Walter

1957   *A Greek–English Lexicon of the New Testament and Other Early Christian Literature*. Trans. William F. Arndt and F. Wilbur Gingrich. Chicago: University of Chicago and Cambridge: Cambridge University Press.

Bauman-Martin, Betsy
2008   'Postcolonial Pollution in the Letter of Jude'. Robert L. Webb and Peter H. Davids, eds. *Reading Jude with New Eyes: Methodological Reassessments of the Letter of Jude*. London: T. & T. Clark, pp. 54-80.

Benjamin, Walter
1968   *Illuminations*. Trans. Harry Zohn. New York: Schocken Books.

Bhabha, Homi K.
1994   *The Location of Culture*. New York: Routledge.

Borges, Jorge Luis
1962   *Ficciones*. Trans. and ed. Anthony Kerrigan. New York: Grove Press, Inc.

Boyarin, Daniel
1999   *Dying for God: Martyrdom and the Making of Judaism and Christianity*. Stanford, CA: Stanford University Press.
2001   'The Gospel of the *Memra*: Jewish Binitarianism and the Prologue to John'. *Harvard Theological Review* 94: 243-84.

Callan, Terrance
2001a 'The Christology of the Second Letter of Peter'. *Biblica* 82: 253-63.
2001b 'The Soteriology of the Second Letter of Peter'. *Biblica* 82: 549-59.
2003   'The Style of the Second Letter of Peter'. *Biblica* 84: 202-24.
2004   'Use of the Letter of Jude by the Second Letter of Peter'. *Biblica* 85: 42-64.
2006   'A Note on 2 Peter 1.19-20'. *Journal of Biblical Literature* 125: 143-50.
2009   'Comparison of Humans to Animals in 2 Peter 2.10b-22'. *Biblica* 90: 101-13.

Cameron, Ron (ed.)
1982   *The Other Gospels*. Philadelphia: The Westminster Press.

Castelli, Elizabeth
1991   *Imitating Paul: A Discourse of Power*. Louisville, KY: Westminster/John Knox Press.

Charles, J. Daryl
2008   'Polemic and Persuasion: Typological and Rhetorical Perspectives on the Letter of Jude'. In Robert L. Webb and Peter H. Davids. (eds.). *Reading Jude with New Eyes: Methodological Reassessments of the Letter of Jude*. London: T. & T. Clark, pp. 81-108.

Chrulew, Matthew N.
2010   *Foucault's Genealogy of Christianity*. PhD dissertation, Monash University, Melbourne, Australia.

Copi, Irving and Carl Cohen
2005　*Introduction to Logic.* Twelfth edition. Upper Saddle River, NJ: Pearson Prentice Hall.

Countryman, L. William
2006　'Jude'. In Deryn Guest, Robert E. Goss, Mona West, and Thomas Bohache. (eds.). *The Queer Bible Commentary.* London: SCM Press, pp. 747-52.

Deleuze, Gilles, and Félix Guattari
1983　*Anti-Oedipus.* Trans. Robert Hurley, Mark Seem, and Helen R. Lane. Minneapolis: University of Minnesota Press.
1986　*Kafka: Toward a Minor Literature.* Trans. Dana Polan. Minneapolis: University of Minnesota Press.
1987　*A Thousand Plateaus.* Trans. Brian Massumi. Minneapolis: University of Minnesota Press.

Deleuze, Gilles
1986　*Cinema 1: The Movement-Image.* Trans. Hugh Tomlinson and Barbara Habberjam. Minneapolis: University of Minnesota Press.
1990　*The Logic of Sense.* Trans. Mark Lester and Charles Stivale. New York: Columbia University Press.

Desjardins, Michel
1987　'The Portrayal of the Dissidents in 2 Peter and Jude: Does It Tell Us More about the 'Godly' than the 'Ungodly'?' *Journal for the Study of the New Testament* 30: 89-102.

Dunn, James D.G.
1994　'Editor's Preface'. In Andrew Chester and Ralph P. Martin, *The Theology of the Letters of James, Peter, and Jude.* Cambridge: Cambridge University Press, pp. ix-x.

Eco, Umberto
1986　*Travels in Hyperreality.* Trans. William Weaver. Orlando, FL: Harcourt Brace Jovanovich.

Ehrman, Bart D.
1993　*The Orthodox Corruption of Scripture.* Oxford: Oxford University Press.
1997　*The New Testament: A Historical Introduction to the Early Christian Writings.* New York: Oxford University Press.

Finney, Jack
1998　*Invasion of the Body Snatchers.* New York: Touchstone Scribner, originally published in 1955 as *The Body Snatchers.*

Frilingos, Christopher A.
2004　*Spectacles of Empire: Monsters, Martyrs, and the Book of Revelation.* Philadelphia: University of Pennsylvania Press.

Gorsline, Robin Hawley
2006 '1 and 2 Peter'. In Deryn Guest, Robert E. Goss, Mona West, and Thomas Bohache. (eds.). *The Queer Bible Commentary*. London: SCM Press, pp. 724-36.

Hayles, N. Katherine
1999 *How We Became Posthuman: Virtual Bodies in Cybernetics, Literature, and Informatics*. Chicago: University of Chicago Press.

Hultin, Jeremy F.
2008 'Bourdieu Reads Jude: Reconsidering the Letter of Jude through Pierre Bourdieu's Sociology'. In Robert L. Webb and Peter H. Davids (eds.). *Reading Jude with New Eyes: Methodological Reassessments of the Letter of Jude*. London: T. & T. Clark, pp. 32-53.

Internet Movie Data Base
2010 Synopsis for *Invasion of the Body Snatchers* (1956). <http.//www.imdb.com/title/tt0049366/synopsis>, accessed 14 March 2010.

Joubert, S.J.
1990 'Language, Ideology and the Social Context of the Letter of Jude'. *Neotestamentica* 24: 335-49.

Joyce, James
1986 *Ulysses*. New York: Random House.

Kafka, Franz
1958 *Parables and Paradoxes*. Various trans. New York: Schocken Books.

Kaufman, Philip (director)
1978 *Invasion of the Body Snatchers*. Los Angeles: United Artists.

Kelly, J.N.D.
1960 *Early Christian Doctrines*. New York: Harper & Row.
1969 *The Epistles of Jude and of Peter*. Harper's New Testament Commentaries. New York: Harper & Row.

Kristeva, Julia
1980 *Desire in Language*. Trans. Thomas Gora, Alice Jardine, and Leon S. Roudiez. New York: Columbia University Press.

Lattimore, Richmond (translator)
1967 *The Odyssey of Homer*. New York: HarperCollins Publishers.

LaValley, Al
1989 *Invasion of the Body Snatchers*. Piscataway, NJ: Rutgers University Press.

Leaney, A.R.C.
1967 *The Letters of Peter and Jude*. The Cambridge Bible Commentary on the New English Bible. Cambridge: Cambridge University Press.

Liddell, Henry George, and Robert Scott.
1996   *A Greek–English Lexicon*. New edition with revised supplement by Henry Stuart Jones and Roderick McKenzie, *et al*. London: Oxford: Clarendon Press.

Martin, Ralph P.
1994   'The Theology of Jude, 1 Peter, and 2 Peter'. In Andrew Chester and Ralph P. Martin. *The Theology of the Letters of James, Peter, and Jude*. Cambridge: Cambridge University Press, pp. 63-163.

Moore, Stephen D.
2000   'Postcolonialism'. In A.K.M. Adam (ed.). *Handbook of Postmodern Biblical Criticism*. St Louis: Chalice Press, pp. 182-88.

Nestle, Eberhard, Erwin Nestle, Kurt Aland, *et al*. (eds.)
1979   *Novum Testamentum Graece*. 26th edition. In *Greek–English New Testament*. Stuttgart: Deutsche Bibelgesellschaft.

Neyrey, Jerome H.
1980   'The Form and Background on the Polemic in 2 Peter'. *Journal of Biblical Literature* 99: 407-31.

Nietzsche, Friedrich
1967   *On the Genealogy of Morals*. Trans. Walter Kaufmann and R.J. Hollingdale. New York: Random House.

Orwell, George (Eric Arthur Blair)
2003   *Nineteen Eighty-Four*. New York: Penguin Plume.

Porter, Stanley E., and Andrew W. Pitts
2008   '*Touto prōton ginōskontes hoti* in 2 Peter 1.20 and Hellenistic Tradition'. *Journal of Biblical Literature* 127: 167-71.

Reese, Ruth Anne
2000   *Writing Jude: The Reader, the Text, and the Author as Constructs of Power and Desire*. Leiden: Brill.

Seesengood, Robert Paul
2007   "Irrational Animals, Bred to Be Caught and Killed': Hybridity, Alterity, and Name-Calling in 2 Peter 2, a Postcolonial Reading'. Unpublished paper, presented to the Society of Biblical Literature, Session on Methodological Reassessments of the Letters of James, Peter, and Jude. San Diego, November 19.

Siegel, Don (director)
1984   *Invasion of the Body Snatchers*. Los Angeles: Allied Artists Pictures (1956). Videotape. Los Angeles: NTA Home Entertainment.

Stills, Stephen (composer)
1966 'For What It's Worth', from the Buffalo Springfield album, *Buffalo Springfield*. Atco Records.

Webb, Robert L.
1996 'The Eschatology of the Epistle of Jude and Its Rhetorical and Social Functions'. *Bulletin for Biblical Research* 6: 139-51.

Webb, Robert L., and Duane F. Watson (eds.).
2010 *Reading Second Peter with New Eyes*. London: T. & T. Clark.

Subject Index

Author Index